Thomas Beckett: Master Saddler

The Story of a Saddlery Business

First published 1994

© **Constance Mary Beckett**

British Library Cataloguing in Publication Data
A catalogue record for this book is available
from the British Library.

ISBN 0 948035 08 0

Published by:
Rushmere Wynne Limited
PO Box 491, Leighton Buzzard
Bedfordshire LU7 7ZS

Printed by:
Redwood Books
Kennet House, Kennet Way
Trowbridge, Wiltshire, BA14 8RN

Edited by John Winters

Thomas Beckett : Master Saddler

The Story of a Saddlery Business

by
Constance Mary Beckett

Rushmere Wynne
England.

FOREWORD

In today's world of commercial giants, supermarkets and chain stores, the idea of a small privately–owned business sounds almost Dickensian.

Yet many such businesses have grown and flourished in this 20th century. This is the story of one of them. For 26 years Thomas Beckett traded successfully in the historic town of Stratford–upon–Avon, having originally started his business in the small Norfolk market town of Thetford.

Jean Adams
October, 1994

ACKNOWLEDGEMENTS

To my sister, Jean Adams, without whom this book would not have been possible. We worked in close collaboration on the early part of the book, recalling childhood memories. I have been fortunate in having the advantage of her valued critical appraisal of my work throughout.

To Harry Drury, my friend and mentor, for his encouragement, help, and generous expertise.

I also owe a great deal of thanks to Olive, Frank and Ethel Beckett, David Moore, Kenneth Boyden, Alan Lewis, Richard Ling, Peter Massey, Fred Stowe, Michael Gillam of Rotary International, and to Stratford-upon-Avon Records Office for all their help during my hours of research.

Contents

PEAK THREE

INTRODUCTION

I invite you to take a walk with me along Wood Street, Stratford-upon-Avon. When you reach the AA shop, turn into Cooks Alley. About halfway down, between the AA shop and Sports Connection, if you are observant, you will notice a sign:

BECKETT HOUSE

"Why Beckett?" you may ask. Well, from 1953 to 1979 the name T. Beckett appeared, in letters of gold, above what is now the AA front window; and over the three box windows in the alley.

From 1932 to 1953 the name could be seen over the bow window that is now J. Jones & Sons.

Who was Thomas Beckett? I have set out to answer that question in my book. My father's business life was made up of a series of peaks, so after the first two chapters, I have divided the rest of my book into these peaks.

Constance Mary Beckett
Stratford-upon-Avon
October 1994

CHAPTER ONE

The Village Lad with a Limp

Thomas Beckett was born at Brant Broughton in Lincolnshire on 28 December, 1888. His mother was a slight, wiry little woman, straight as a ramrod, in nature as in figure. She was neat, precise, and business-like. Her dark hair was drawn tightly back from her face and forehead into a bun at the nape of her neck. Her children used to tease her, when she was busy about the house, or in the kitchen cooking their meals. "Mind your hair doesn't get in your eyes, Mother." There was little chance of that!

Harriet Beckett, the matriach, who died
26 August 1926, aged 77

She was not just an efficient housewife. She was postmistress and manageress of the village shop. Cottage accommodation was one of the perks of the job. It was from this remarkable little mother that Tom was later to inherit his aptitude for business. His father was the village carrier. He was a big man - easy going, lovable, and more than willing to leave the management of the home, family and shop to his efficient wife. She was the matriach.

Unlike the healthy children, brother William, sister Bess, and Bob, who later died at sea, Tom started life at a physical disadvantage. As a baby, Thomas was afflicted with poliomyelitis - or infantile paralysis as it was called in those days. He was to go through life crippled, with a deformed foot, and one leg shorter than the other.

As a child, he would hobble to school supported by a little walking stick. However, by break time, when the stiffness had worn off, his crutch became a useful weapon. He would brandish it in self-defence against any who dare mock his disability. In later life he was to become acquainted with his wife's uncle, known to his friends as Uncle Merry. This delightful little shoemaker was to design beautifully-personalised boots for Tom, giving him comfort and support. The one boot built up, for the lame leg to match the length of the other. Thomas loved his mother dearly, but he was a real boy, and not always co-operative. He was never openly rebellious, but not past using a little harmless cunning to serve his purpose. Mrs Beckett, determined to instil some culture into her son, insisted on music lessons for him. Thomas was not destined to be a pianist of any kind, let alone a musical genius. Hence, when his mother went to market leaving him at the piano, he quickly escaped to more congenial pursuits. He employed a friendly neighbour to warn him of mother's approach, thus giving him time to return demurely to The Bluebells of Scotland.

By the time Thomas had reached the age of 14, it was apparent to his wise little mother that her delicate son, with his physical disability, was ill-equipped for the hard and robust life of a farm labourer. Indeed, he would never be fit to find employment in the agricultural community. Her practical mind told her that Tom should seek an apprenticeship, and learn a trade. She broached the subject with her husband. He also wanted the best for Tom. He agreed with her proposition, as always, knowing he only had to acquiesce, and she would make the necessary contacts and arrangements. Thus, it came about that Tom was apprenticed to the saddler, John Henry Holderness of Sleaford.

The old almshouses in Brant Broughton, Lincolnshire where Grandma Beckett finished her days.

The Methodist Chapel in Brant Broughton where Thomas Beckett worshipped

In the summer of 1938 the author and her parents spent a weekend at Brant Broughton, where they shared the Sunday School Anniversary celebrations. The family is standing with friends in front of a horse-drawn dray which took the children all round the village singing their anniversary hymns. The members of the family in the picture are (left), Thomas Beckett's nephew, Frank Beckett; Thomas; (fourth from right) Constance Mary Beckett, the author; Bessie Beckett, Thomas's sister; and (right) Edith Beckett.

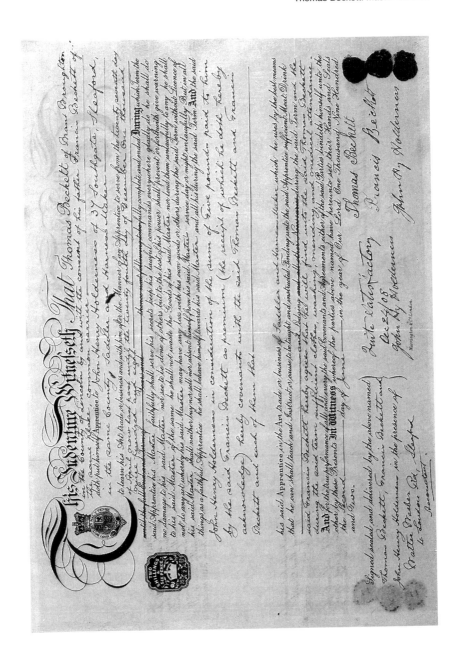

The indentures of apprenticeship for Thomas Beckett

Thomas Beckett (third from right, front row) pictured in his Sunday School class at the age of seven.

Thomas Beckett, aged about 12. The star at the end of the gold chain was a Sunday School award for good conduct and punctuality.

CHAPTER TWO

Kettering and Grantham

After seven years' apprenticeship, Tom was now a qualified Master Saddler. He went to work at Kettering as a journeyman. It was at Kettering that he met his future wife. Edith Moore was an employee of Kettering Co-operative Society. She worked in the factory as a tailoress, mastering her trade as thoroughly as her husband-to-be had mastered his.

The Moore family were Methodists. They belonged to the Rockingham Road Church. Edith's brother, Arthur, came home from a mid-week meeting one night, and announced that a new young man had joined the church at Rockingham Road. "He's taken a job at Old Hardys the Saddler, in Market Street," he informed the family. Edith and her friends were all agog to inspect the newcomer. When they did set eyes on Arthur's latest contact, Edith turned to her friend, and said "I'm going to marry that man." And she did. Of course, it took a little time for the shy young Lincolnshire lad to realise that he was targeted. However, the next few months were to prove that he was not indifferent to the charms of this determined young lady, who was to become his life partner, supporting him through good and bad times in his business and church career.

His first gift to her was a suede leather bag, two-handled, and cunningly fringed round the top. His own creation, of course. The engagement present, purchased with hard-earned savings, was a beautiful gold watch. She wore and treasured it for more than 40 years. (Sadly, it disappeared with the loot taken by burglars when our house in Luddington Road, Stratford-upon-Avon was broken into while our parents were working at the shop at 45a Wood Street).

19

Tom and Edith were married on 23 September, 1915. It was a white wedding, but somewhat subdued by the restrictions imposed by the First World War. They went to live in Grantham, where Tom had got himself a job with Frank Lamb, as Saddler and General Assistant.

Edith was a good, resourceful housekeeper. On a Saturday night she would go down to the market with her shopping basket, and fill it with meat and vegetables, bought at bargain prices. Tom's wife was always smartly dressed, but she was not extravagant. She made most of her own clothes, and the fabrics she chose were remnants or materials bought in a sale. As Methodists, the young couple were teetotallers. Their social life was mainly satisfied by events connected with the Finkin Street Methodist Church.

I was born on 8 July, 1917. Weekends should have been happy, relaxing times when Edith and Tom could enjoy each other's company, but Tom was a local preacher. Some Sundays he would be away all day. He would conduct a service at one of the villages in the morning; have lunch with the chapel steward or one of the members, then take the evening service at a nearby village. So Edith spent many lonely Sabbaths with only a squalling child for company.

Those early days of married life were quite a struggle. Tom worked long hours, and never refused to do a little overtime in the busy harvest season. He was glad of the extra money. On the home front, Edith valiantly tackled the problem of housekeeping and looking after the child. In those days there were no play schools to give a young mother a few hours' respite from child-caring. Edith loved her little girl, but I am told I was not a restful child. Mother made me a little brown overall creeping suit. Once I began to walk unsteadily, she needed to keep a constant eye upon me. Father had planted a few vegetables in the small back garden. One day I could not be found. Mother searched all over the house, then came downstairs, and went into the garden. There, moving among the cabbages was a brown object, a little too slow and too large for a rabbit. Just a happy brown child!

Apparently I was a somewhat adventurous toddler. On one occasion I chose a rainy day to explore the garden. When mother discovered me, I was caked in mud and slime from head to foot. She had the water heated in the old-fashioned copper in the kitchen, ready to tackle the weekly wash. However, instead of the washing, she dumped me wholesale into the copper, and soaked off my sodden dirty garments. When she ultimately came to the squealing, naked child, she vigorously applied a bar of Sunlight Soap.

By the year 1920, memories of war were fading, and tensions lessening, both nationally and domestically. At the beginning of this new decade there was a general air of optimism and hope. Tom was very conscious of his responsibility as a family man, with a two-year-old daughter, and another child on the way. In those days, the firm's reps were pretty good judges of a man's capabilities. On their rounds to their saddlery customers, they would meet the workers. Many of these young men were excellent craftsmen, but sadly, did not possess the qualities that would ensure success in running their own businesses. Others showed promise as potential shopkeepers.

The reps, discussing these matters amongst themselves, generally placed young Tom Beckett in the latter category. "Ever thought of going into business on your own, Tom?" a friendly rep asked him one day. Consequently, Tom began to think along these lines. It was an attractive prospect. He went home and discussed the matter with his wife, whose judgement he valued, with good reason. Edith was never merely supportive. She would frequently take the initiative, thus proving herself the ideal partner for a man of Tom's gentle easy-going disposition. Neither of them had any business experience. The world of commerce was new to them. But they were a practical pair, and faced the fact that even if the right business for them came on the market, their slender savings could never amount to the capital required to launch it.

This obstacle was uppermost in their minds when Tom was attracted to a shop advertised in his trade journal. The reps encouraged him to go for this shop situated in the centre of the market town of Thetford in Norfolk. I shall always believe that it was thanks to the initial generosity of the wholesale firm Eldrid Ottaway & Co., of 48 Whitecross Street, London, that Tom became the successful man he was to prove himself to be. Their faith in him, expressed practically in the offer of a loan of £100, was the Godsend that the young people needed. They accepted with gratitude.

Once they were launched at Thetford, Tom's main concern was to pay back the money, which he did, within 12 months.

Thomas Beckett at the age of 20 pictured with his bicycle.

Thomas and Edith pictured on their wedding day in September, 1915. Edith had her 23rd birthday the previous month and Thomas was 27 the following December.

PEAK ONE

CHAPTER THREE

Thetford

Tom travelled to Thetford to view the business advertised in his trade journal. And what good business premises they appeared to be. A double-fronted shop, with living quarters attached. But what living quarters! That, Edith was to discover later. She had left a small, but cosy, compact house with a manageable garden in Grantham. When she arrived in Thetford she was pregnant and tired of coping with an over-active three-year-old. She was confronted with this large, grey, three-storey tenement-like building in a narrow, busy street near a river. Inside the house she found a pantry as large as most people's kitchen; a coal-house; a kitchen containing an old-fashioned boiler; and a black-leaded range. There were eight large rooms in total, with numerous cupboards, all at different levels. There were stairs and steps everywhere. The grounds were equally large, rambling and inconvenient. The rear windows of the house looked out on to a dark, sun-less yard. It contained stables, store-rooms, a brick pig-sty and outhouses of every description, which Tom saw as potential work-rooms, garage space and storage units. Beyond the yard was a long walled garden at the top of which was a wash-house! How many weary steps from the main house - all of which added up to a children's paradise and a mother's nightmare?

The workroom was a vital part of the business. Our workman, Freddie Wells, had ample space in the huge area above the store-room next to the house. Here, harnesses for farm horses were repaired. The saddler's shop soon became an emporium where local requirements were met and from where a variety of merchandise could be obtained. We were proud of the claim, frequently made: *You're sure to find it at Becketts.* Whenever there was a demand, Thomas would supply. He was a careful buyer. He felt his way, particularly with new lines, increasing his stock only when there was a steady demand. He soon discovered that there was no upholsterer in Thetford, hence it was not long before the spacious workroom began to assume the appearance of a secondhand furnishing depot. Another of his skills was repairing bellows. I can visualise him now sitting tapping in the tiny gold-coloured nails to anchor the leather stretched around the bellows. It was a beautiful piece of craftsmanship.

Then Thomas opened an account with the Ever Ready Company. It was a brilliant move.

The sale of torches, batteries, and bulbs went up and up. To introduce variety to the torch trade, he later stocked Pifco products. At Christmas-time they produced charming little scenes illuminated from inside. They made delightful gifts, and were a joy to sell.

One day, our parents went to Norwich. The following morning a large delivery van turned into the yard entrance beside the shop. We watched the expert furniture-removers lift a beautiful display unit out of the van. The side wall opposite the counter in the shop had been cleared to receive the handsome addition to our simple shop furniture. It was a mahogany, glass-fronted unit set on deep wooden drawers, bought at a sale of shopfittings from Boots the Chemists in Norwich. As the new Christmas stock came in, the handbags and leather goods were stored and displayed in this newly-acquired fixture. It was a tremendous boost to Christmas trade, and a pleasure to behold. Such improvements were made gradually when the cash-flow permitted.

We children loved the months coming up to Christmas when the stock was stored in a spare room upstairs. We spent hours in that room, playing with the games that would be other children's Christmas presents. These were priced at:

Ordinary sets	6 $\frac{1}{2}$d and 1s.
Superior sets	2s 6d
Very special sets	5s.

All were supplied by the Glevum Works, Gloucester.

I fear a few of the sets were slightly secondhand when we had finished with them!

*Thomas Beckett's shop in Bridge Street, Thetford,
which changed little in appearance between 1920 and 1932, the 12 years the Becketts traded there.*

Another venture was the introduction of Standard Fireworks. They were displayed in the glass counter-top on the sales side, opposite the Boots display unit. Cannons, rockets, snow-storms, catherine wheels, Prince of Wales feathers, and sparklers looked exciting and colourful under the glass.

Beckett's also ran a fireworks club. The lads would pay so much a week, then collect their fireworks on 5th November. To house these flammable goods, I remember the fireproof iron safe being installed in the area under the stairs leading to the workroom. It was typical of our parents that they kept the profit from the firework sales separate from the general takings. It was reserved for purchasing new fittings for the shop.

* * * *

We were very proud of being the children of a master saddler. We were unique. Our toys were not bought from ordinary toy shops. Father made leather toys for us. One of our favourites was Wilfred, a rabbit, with long leather ears. He was stuffed with saddle wool, and was remarkably good-tempered. He never looked any the worse for our occasional ill-treatment of the poor animal.

Mother was always very much involved in the business, often serving in the shop. She was, in fact, a kind of unpaid part-time shop assistant. With two small children and a large house to run, domestic help was necessary. Our maids were kindly and long-suffering. At one time we employed a lovely girl called Doris. She adored my pretty mischievous little sister. When Doris got down on her knees to polish the floor, Jean gleefully climbed on her back. Doris thought this was wonderful, until she had completed her task, shed the child and stood up. She would put her hand to the back of her head and discover that her straight black hair had been tied into tight little knots by the angelic child...

Then there was the girl who had long black hair, taken back into a thick splendid plait. Needless to say, little Jean amused herself tugging this tempting rope of hair, whenever she could catch it. For no reason that I can remember, we christened this girl Polixophus.

28

Jean Beckett at the age of two pictured with
sister Constance Mary, who was five.

Thomas and Edith Beckett pictured with their two daughters,
by which time Jean was five and her sister, eight.

Freddie Wells and Thomas Beckett in the workroom at Thetford busy on the saddles which were such an important part of the business.

CHAPTER FOUR

The River Thet and a Cluster of Anecdotes

In an angry mood, when the heavy rains came, the River Thet burst its banks. The water flowed unchecked down Bridge Street. The efforts of the shopkeepers to stem the flow with sandbags were in vain. The water soon reached the step of our shop and flowed along the passage into the dining room, right through the house. I remember Father lifting us children to safety on the large dining room table. We watched the water rushing down the steep step, and cascading round the legs of the table.

When the water subsided, scrubbing up operations began. In spite of vigorous efforts on the part of Mother and Polixophus to cleanse the house, it was many months before the dank, stale river smell cleared. This unhealthy atmosphere was particularly harmful to Mother, whose resistance, in any case, was low.

Bridge Street, Thetford showing the river bridge and St. Peter's Church.

The river presented a much happier aspect at the time of the annual carnival. As dusk fell, it came into its own, with gaily-illuminated boats floating under the bridge. During the day local tradesmen paraded their wares on colourful and imaginative floats. Father was always happy to enter, with enthusiasm, into any of the town's activities; and, of course, to grasp an opportunity to advertise his goods. Weeks of preparation went into the task of devising and constructing a suitable, topical and representative decorative display. I remember on one occasion the car was transformed into a miniature tennis court. Jean and I were balanced precariously either side of the net, brandishing tennis rackets. In these constructions Father was willingly assisted by our friend, Mr Munns, the Manager of Turner's shoe shop in the High Street.

The Beckett's car is decorated ready for the carnival.

* * * *

There was a large pear tree at the bottom of the garden. We loved it. Father fixed a swing on one of the tough lower boughs. When life at ground level became boring, we clambered up into the higher branches, often taking our toys with us, and forming our own little playhouse. The harvest of pears in the autumn was abundant. The attic provided ample space in which to ripen them. As we sometimes slept in the next room, it was very tempting to pop next door for a midnight feast. Squashed pear on bare feet was a small price to pay for such illicit pleasures.

One particularly good vintage year, a skip full of juicy pears was placed enticingly outside the shop, bearing the notice:

HELP YOURSELF

We children concealed ourselves just inside the shop-door so that we could peep out and watch the delighted people 'helping themselves'. First a man and woman came along. They looked at the notice, looked at each other, looked round suspiciously, looked back at the notice - and walked on! The only pears taken that day were whipped by a couple of schoolboys, who failed to read the notice, and congratulated themselves on a piece of successful scrumping! The rest of the public evidently considered that if it was free, it must be suspect.

By nightfall, only the 'stolen' fruit was missing. Father hauled the skip in. Next day our resident pigs enjoyed an enormous feast, thanks to the humans who spurned our generous gesture.

Jean in the pear tree.

There were several large estates in the area. Where there were estates, there were horses, and where there were horses, saddlers were needed.

Although Thursday was half-day closing for the local shops, it was not a leisure afternoon for the Becketts. Tom and Edith drove out into the country to take orders and collect and deliver repairs. Whenever school permitted, we children loved to accompany them on these expeditions.

We set off in the old Singer car. I should explain that father was one of the few local businessmen to own a car. His disability made this acquisition necessary. Jean and I would be squeezed into the back seat. She would be propped up by an upturned riding saddle. I was equally wedged in by harnesses needing repair. I can still recall the horsy smell of the bridles and head-collars wrapped around my feet. We visited farms, stables and local estates.

On one occasion Lord Fisher ordered a member of his staff: "Give these girls two guinea pigs." Fortunately for us, we had an indulgent father. Hence, on arriving home, weary as he was after a busy time with the clients, he patiently rooted out a suitable wooden box and fixed a wire netting covered run for the new pets.

The Becketts return to Thetford in their car,
complete with the guinea pigs.

We soon discovered that they were male and female. So they began to increase at an alarming rate. School-friends were supplied with baby guinea pigs until parents began to protest. Eventually, our long-suffering mother was driven to surreptitiously make little escape routes in the wire netting. After we children had gone to bed, of course!

Tibby was a tiny grey kitten who was tremendously curious. He would sit for hours on the shop doorstep, watching the traffic go by. One day he went missing. We searched all his favourite haunts, glanced anxiously across the narrow, busy street, but found no pathetic little corpse to justify our worst fears. At the end of a worrying day, a boy from the nearby Grammar School came into the shop carrying a small wet, bedraggled kitten. Apparently Tibby's curiosity had got the better of him. He had wandered down to the river, and fallen in. Father thankfully received him and gave the lad sixpence as a reward. So was that the end of the story? Not quite. It seemed that our hero related the story of the rescue to his fellow pupils, naturally not omitting the reward.

Unfortunately, some of his enterprising, but less scrupulous pals decided that they could be on to a good thing. Abducting Tibby became quite a popular sport. He was always returned, slightly damp, but otherwise unharmed. Father was too canny to be taken in for long and when the sixpences were no longer forthcoming, Tibby's adventures came to an abrupt end.

Sadly, his next disappearance did not end happily. We found his little body under the firework safe in an outhouse where he had crept away to die. Someone had been careless about laying rat poison.

Tibby.

There were times when we did court disaster. As the interest in tennis increased, the question was naturally asked: "Where do we play?" The problem was running around Tom's mind when he happened to meet a friend of his, an Anglican clergyman who was a keen tennis-player. The outcome of that meeting was a proposition that Tom and the Vicar should go into partnership to cater for Thetford and district tennis-players.

Plans went forward to lay two hard courts on Brandon Road, a mile out of town. It appeared to be an amicable arrangement. However, the Vicar stipulated that the court should not be let on Good Friday or Saints' days. Tom, the good Methodist, was totally opposed to letting the court on the Sabbath. Both men were true to their principles. Unfortunately, this was not conducive to good business, as each stipulated closure on the most popular days. It was apparent at the outset that the use of the court would be limited, even though the Vicar promised to advertise widely to his sporting friends.

After two years' struggle to make it pay, both partners agreed that the venture had failed, and decided to cut their losses. Even we children, who had enjoyed playing on the court - free of charge, of course - were glad to see it go, as we nearly always had to brush and roll it before we could play.

One memory of this ill-fated court stands out vividly. Our lovely Airedale bitch, Nip, had just had puppies. As a special treat, we took her in the car to the courts so that she had the space to run and let herself go after her confinement. So intoxicated was she with her freedom that she tore round in utter abandonment and ran straight under the wheels of a motor-cycle. Her back was broken. A tearful visit to the vet confirmed our worst fears. He assured us that the only humane thing to do was to let him put her down. We managed to rear the one puppy we kept, with a bottle tucked through an old fur coat. He grew to be a really lovable dog, but nothing could ever quite replace our dear Nip in our affections.

Thomas Beckett with Nip.

CHAPTER FIVE

Happy Years at Thetford

The 12 years at Thetford were happy and successful ones. The business prospered. Our parents' hard work and dedication were rewarded. However, it was not all work. Tom and Edith entered into the life of the community. The whole family was involved in the worship and social events of the Methodist chapel in Tanners Street. We children fancied ourselves as little starlets, perched up on the platform at the Sunday School Anniversary, saying our recitations. Mother, who had taken elocution lessons in her younger days, put us through our paces with great thoroughness. We were encouraged to memorise not only poetry, but great chunks of the Scriptures. Sometimes we were allowed to take part in services conducted in one of the villages by Father.

Mother soon became popular as a performer when she joined the local concert party. Her pianist was a great friend of the family. He supplied the musical accompaniment to Mother's monologues. We were immensely proud of her. When she appeared on the stage at the Town Hall, we kids nudged the school pals sitting next to us. "That's our Mother." She always had an encore, often more than one. It was wonderful. She wore the most stunning dresses - home-made, of course.

Her glorious contralto voice made her a welcome member of the augmented church choir, when they presented oratorios at Easter, Christmas and on other special occasions. Father was a modest man. He was proud of us, but he would stay in the background, often observing "Three Becketts on show is more than sufficient for one family". My sister was pretty and dainty, quite the little fairy. She was frequently chosen to present the bouquet to the lady opener at the church bazaar or local garden fete.

We might have gone on living at Thetford for many years, had it not been for Mother's deteriorating health. Thetford did not suit her. We were too near the river, for one thing. On her not-so-good days, when she had to succumb and stay in bed, we were most unhappy and frightened.

On one of these occasions, I remember praying most urgently "Oh, God, don't let Mummy die." Early in the year of 1932, when I was 14 and Jean 11, Mother had a very serious illness. On her doctor's advice, Father came to a decision. We must move from Thetford. No matter how we prospered, Mother's health came first. Then began the search for a new business.

Father carefully studied the sales page in his monthly trade journal, *Leathergoods*. Of course, the rep 'grapevine' was a valuable source of information. By the time various possibilities were being considered, Mother was well enough to take a lively interest in the proceedings.

The prospect of leaving Thetford and enjoying better health did much to restore her. Hence, our parents travelled all over the country inspecting businesses. It was very exciting. Where were we going? They were impressed by the superb premises of a shop at Bexhill-on-Sea and tempted to go ahead with negotiations to obtain it. Then the Stratford-upon-Avon business came on to the market. The reps reported that the owner, Harold Fry, had personal problems that were responsible for some recent neglect, hence his desire to quit. They told Father that the business in its present state was a challenge, but assured him that the potential was great.

The main task would be to restore customer confidence. So serious negotiations began with the said Mr Fry. Our parents decided to go and have a look at the shop. Harold Fry, somewhat cunningly, arranged for them to inspect the shop on a Bank Holiday Monday, when the town was packed with visitors. That visit was the deciding factor. Negotiations went ahead. The transaction was ultimately completed.

My father took over the business at 45a Wood Street. He found lodgings with a pleasant lady, Mrs Kemp, in Birmingham Road. Then he began to look around for a house for the family.

Mother was left to clear things up at 8 Bridge Street, Thetford. I had left school at the end of the Spring term. Jean had been packed off to Kettering to live at Gran's until we all moved to Stratford. I remember watching Mother go through the ledger one day. She frowned. "All these unpaid bills. We must try and get them in." "We?" I blinked. "Yes, you can help me."

I was flattered. I suppose, in a way, this marked the beginning of my career as a business girl. Mother made a list of the outstanding debts, then we started our unpopular purge on debtors.

We were so remorseless with our threatening letters and persistent, demanding phone calls that by the time the business was transferred to Father's faithful workman, Freddie Wells, nearly all the bad debts had been collected. When Father found a house for us in Luddington Road, Mother joined him and I was taken to Kettering.

Mr Rudd, Freddie Wells and Thomas Beckett pictured during the Thetford period.

PEAK TWO - 45a WOOD STREET

CHAPTER SIX

Stratford-upon-Avon

Thomas Beckett faced and met a challenge when he bought his first business at Thetford. The Stratford-upon-Avon shop presented a new and different kind of challenge. For instance, the stock he had bought from his predecessor was low, and gave little indication as to the type and quality of merchandise needed to meet the demands of his new - and as yet unknown - clientele. As in the early days at Thetford, he had to feel his way. Mistakes were made in buying. With the intention of establishing Becketts as a luggage shop, the rather tired-looking six suitcases taken over from Mr Fry were replaced by a large consignment of modestly-priced fibre cases. They didn't sell. Unlike Thetford, the demand in Stratford-upon-Avon was for better quality luggage.

Gradually, the right brands were introduced. First the Antler range (J.B.Brooks). Then the more expensive Victor models. Executive and folio cases were mostly produced by our Walsall 'houses'.* Similarly, the buying of sports equipment went through the upgrading process.

The sales area was, of course, only part of the business, but it was the part of the business that to the general population of Stratford had the highest profile. We were practical saddlers and the floor above the Henley Street shop was a large workroom. The repair service team of three continued to work under the new management. The experienced Arthur Trotman and Tom Goode were also training the young saddler, John Rimel, who much later was to launch into business on his own at Shipston-on-Stour.

* *'houses' refers to manufacturers.*

43

Est. 1851. 'PHONE 233

WILLIAM HYATT 45a, Wood Street,
(T. Beckett). and 66 Henley Street,

Stratford-on-Avon.

June 1st, 1932.

Dear Sir or Madam,

I beg to inform you I have this day taken over the old established, and well-known business of Mr. William Hyatt, at the above addresses, and have re-engaged the staff of experienced workmen.

You may rely on the same first-class workmanship and quality of goods as well as prompt attention to all orders, by which means I trust to merit a continuance of your patronage and support in the future.

Your obedient Servant,

T. BECKETT.

One of the letters sent out in June 1932 by Thomas Beckett to advise customers of the William Hyatt business formerly owned by Harold Fry that he had become the new owner.

A month after the takeover, I arrived on the scene. It was especially exciting for me as it marked the real beginning of my business career. I was fascinated by the shop, or rather two shops with frontage in Wood Street and another frontage in Henley Street. So different from the traditional double-fronted Thetford premises. The Wood Street side was (and still is) charming, but dark, with its beautiful Tudor beams and low ceiling. Here one had to work under artificial light all day. The Henley Street side was (and still is) lofty, light, airy and comparatively modern. A most unusual marriage of architecture embracing a single business unit.

The one thing that did not please me was the Wood Street window. It was old-fashioned, poky, indeed, most unsatisfactory. Being high and shallow, however cunningly goods were displayed, it looked cluttered and unprofessional. It was most frustrating. However, within a few years, Father applied for and was granted permission to fit a new bow window.

It was a vast improvement. Not only was it easily accessible, the shape was ideal for displaying our particular type of merchandise.

The new bow window fitted to the Wood Street frontage
of the Stratford–upon–Avon shop.

One of the exciting things about trading in Stratford-upon-Avon was doing business with the recently-opened Shakespeare Memorial Theatre. The old theatre was burnt down in 1926. Property Manager Kegan Smith soon discovered that the new owner of the leather goods shop in Wood Street could be relied upon to meet the urgent, often impatient demands of the producers of the plays. Phone calls to Walsall houses for express delivery of belts, sword frogs etc, were frequent; particularly in the seasons when the Shakespearean histories were presented. The sight of Kegan, or one of his staff, charging into the shop, waving a theatre order pad, became a familiar one. The answer to the stock question "When do you require these goods?" was a breathless "Yesterday. He's on our tail. There's a dress rehearsal tonight. Please do your best."

If the item was something we could deal with in our own workshop, one of our workmen would be taken off the job he was doing and given the urgent theatre job. Otherwise, it was a hot line to one of our Walsall houses. They were co-operative to the extent that one of their supervisors would invariably get into his car and bring the goods over, rather than trust them to the post or British Railways.

Beckett's also supplied the theatre cricket club enthusiastically captained by Trevor Howard. Privately, members of the company patronised Beckett's shop. Michael Redgrave and several members of his family bought their tennis rackets from Beckett's. John Slater would come loping into the Henley Street shop, grab a box of tennis balls from the shelf between the two shops and on his way out to Wood Street, shout over his shoulder "I'll call in and pay tomorrow."

The late John Slater, pictured in the 1930s. He would come loping into the Henley Street shop to grab a box of tennis balls.

46

Tomorrow and tomorrow and tomorrow. Since tomorrow never came, several reminders of the debt had to be handed in to the stage door office before it was paid.

Norman Wooland was off back to London at the end of the season leaving an unpaid bill of 17s. 7d. Once we discovered his address, we despatched an account with a sharp reminder that the bill was overdue. Instead of a cheque for the amount owing, we received this letter that is worth recording in full for its sheer audacity.

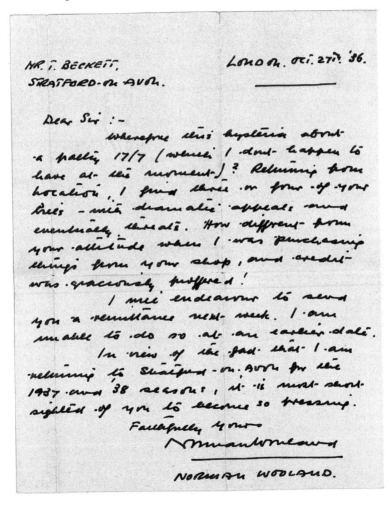

The letter Thomas Beckett received from Norman Wooland.

During the 1930s, actors were poorly paid and so tended to seek credit from local tradesmen. One young actor, whose name never hit the headlines, chose in mid-season a cabin trunk, ready for use when he travelled back to London at the end of the season. He paid by instalments - £1 a month from his pay packet. Thirty shillings was still owing. Mr Beckett agreed to deliver the trunk, on condition that the final settlement was made the following day.

Two days before the company was due to depart, the debt was still not paid. I was so annoyed about this, I stalked off to his lodgings and rang the door bell. When the landlady opened the door, I asked if I might have a word with her lodger. It was some time before he responded to the call.

Like Viola, I stood my ground. Ultimately he appeared, somewhat sheepishly. I handed the bill to him and demanded payment there and then. Abashed, the young man slowly removed his wallet from an inner pocket in his jacket, drew out a £1 note, then a ten shilling note and reluctantly handed them to his tormenter. I accepted the money briskly, bade him a bright "Good day and thank you" and went. Mission painfully accomplished. I actually felt quite sorry for him.

One of Beckett's enterprising small firms produced a collection of leather goods shaped like books. Shaving sets, jewel cases and handbags were cleverly camouflaged to look as if they belonged to a library shelf. On the various coloured morocco spines of these cream luxonhide 'books', were titles of Shakespeare's plays embossed in gold lettering. Perhaps the most popular play in the 1950 season was *Much Ado About Nothing* with John Gielgud (now Sir John) and Peggy Ashcroft playing the leading roles of Benedick and Beatrice.

The late Dame Peggy Ashcroft,
so nice to have this famous
actress's autograph – on a cheque.

This happy production was chosen for the last night of the season. As chance would have it, Becketts still had in stock a book shaving set bearing the name of the play. It seemed the perfect gift for Peggy Ashcroft to present to her Benedick, John Gielgud. Hence, a message was phoned through to the theatre. On receiving this, Miss Ashcroft came down to the shop to inspect this unique piece of merchandise. She was enchanted with it and graciously thanked our firm for bringing it to her notice. Nice to be able to anticipate the needs of a grateful purchaser. Nicer still to have this famous actress's autograph - on a cheque.

Earlier in the season, we had been honoured by a visit from John Gielgud, when he bought a dog harness and collar for his cocker spaniel. A few days after the purchase, a taxi driver brought the harness back to exchange it for a larger size. He told us that he drove the actor back to Chipping Camden every night after his performance at the theatre. The driver's admiration for his famous 'fare' was unbounded. "A smashing fellow. A real gentleman."

Sir John Gielgud, who bought a dog harness and collar for his cocker spaniel.

Keith Michell was another satisfied customer. As well as being a popular and successful member of the company, he was a keen horseman who enjoyed riding as a break from acting. It was a great thrill for our firm when he came into the shop and ordered a horse-rug to be made to his own specification. Our Walsall saddlery firm, D. Mason & Sons, made a magnificent job of this truly Shakespearean horse-rug. It was black, with yellow cadis binding, a motif of rosemary on one side and the initials K.M. on the other.

Another unusual request came from the Fossett's Circus. Mr Fossett, the owner of this small, local concern, came into the shop one day, with a lovely young girl, a member of his troupe. She needed a leather mould to protect and strengthen her mouth for her act of swinging through the air, hanging on only by her clenched teeth. Father's ingenuity was tested to the limit. However, having no professional dental equipment, he compromised by using a hunk of bread on which she bit, so forming an impression of her palate. From this he was able to build up the required leather mould.

Fitting bits into the mouths of big, champing horses had never given him quite the satisfaction he derived from creating a mouth-piece for this pretty little filly!

Special orders were welcomed, not only from the theatre, but also from the Salvation Army. Reg Jones, an old Stratfordian and life-long Salvationist, recalls the time when his double B flat base instrument - the largest in the band, he told me - became too heavy for him to carry. He automatically took the problem to Mr Beckett. Subsequently, two strong straps for the shoulders and waist were made to his requirements and the instrument became manageable again.

The bandsmen all carried black leather pouches. When, after years of service, they began to show signs of wear, Reg said to his companions "I'll go along and see Mr Beckett. I'm sure he will be able to copy the design."

They were duly proudly kitted out with tough new hide pouches, made to measure. When Reg told me this story, he added with a smile "I've still got mine." Although Mr Beckett was the owner of the business, employing three workmen (Arthur Trotman, Tom Goode and John Rimel) he was still recognised as a practical saddler who could perform near-miracles on leather. The late Donald Wolfit treated him as a consultant for his personal theatre requirements. Mr Beckett had more than just a pleasant business relationship with him. The Wolfit family hailed from Brant Broughton. Two of his sisters still lived in Thomas Beckett's native village. Donald Wolfit would often come into the shop for a chat with his fellow Lincolnshire countryman. So it was not surprising that he should seriously request the master saddler to take the annoying squeak out of his Hamlet shoes.

For many years, Baliol Holloway was an essential part of the Stratford scene throughout the Shakespearean season. As also was Tony, his constant canine companion. 'Bay' soon found his way to the shop that could supply Tony's new dog collar. When he returned to London at the end of the Shakespearean season, Tony's sartorial needs were met by post. In fact, Beckett's supplied Tony's collars and leads for the rest of his doggie life. When he died in 1948, at the ripe old age of 15, Bay was broken-hearted. For a while he would not consider a successor. Then one day, he was walking by Sadlers Wells Theatre when he came across a pathetic little stray puppy, hungry and obviously homeless. The kind-hearted actor took the poor little creature to a police station from where he was sent to the Battersea Dogs Home. Bay visited him every day for a week. When no-one claimed him, Bay became his new master. That marked the beginning of a new life for the six-month-old stray who, as Bay put it, "had evidently been chucked out on the street because his licence was due". The pup was named Joey, after Joseph Grimaldi, the famous clown of olden days, who played at the 'Wells'.

Baliol Holloway with Tony.

Needless to say, Beckett's had the honour of being appointed Joey's Saville Row. We were rather amused, and not a little flattered, when Bay's request for a dog lead with a scissor clip, was accompanied by the comment "I got one at Selfridge's, but it was awful muck. Made from brown paper, I think, and the clip doesn't hold".

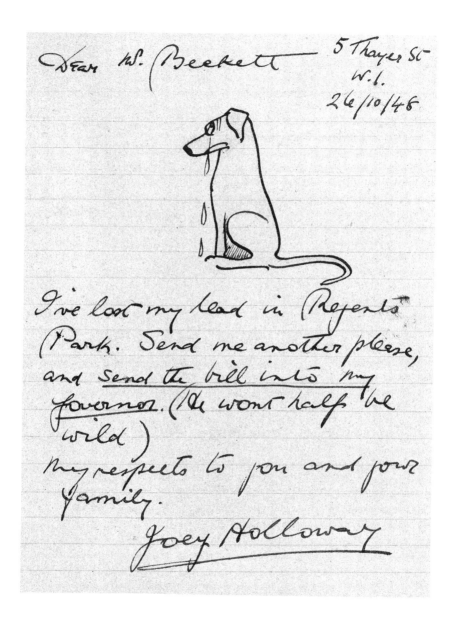

Dear Mr. Beckett — 5 Thayer St
W.1.
26/10/48

I've lost my lead in Regents
Park. Send me another please,
and send the bill into my
governor. (He wont half be
wild)
My respects to you and your
family.

Joey Holloway

Letter from Joey (Baliol) Holloway

CHAPTER SEVEN

Advertising
and Window Dressing

Throughout the 1930s and in the early war years we advertised in our local newspaper, the *Stratford-upon-Avon Herald*. Every Tuesday morning I would trundle along to 29 High Street with my copy to be printed in the *Herald* that was then published on a Friday.

In those days the *Herald* office was unimpressive. It was reached along a narrow passage between the International Stores and Jaeger, then up 19 steps to a small office. This limited space housed the printing press and some paper was stored in an attic - a climb of another seven steps.

No wonder we paid only seven shillings for a 2in double column on the front page! It was not until April 1948 that Mr George Boyden bought York House Hotel when it was auctioned at the Town Hall. Then the *Herald* office was transferred to its present splendid premises.

As we gained confidence, we began to introduce new lines. One summer's day a gentleman came into the shop. After he had made his purchase, he looked around and seemed to be focusing his attention on the doggie requisites. He began chatting to my father, explaining that he was on holiday. He was a Devonshire man. Suddenly he said: "Have you ever thought of stocking dog baskets?" Then he went on to explain: "I represent a firm that makes rustic dog baskets. It's a kind of cottage industry at Braunton in Devon. We are a small firm - we only supply two retailers at present and we have no outlet in this part of the country." After some discussion, my father agreed to "try half-a-dozen". They arrived a few weeks later.

There was a little nook outside, to the left of the bow window, that

Some examples of the local newspaper advertisements devised
by the author to promote the family business.

54

55

seemed designed for the display of dog baskets. We found a suitable box on which we stacked three different models.

They attracted immediate attention and were sold in no time. Repeat orders were promptly executed. We must have sold thousands of baskets over our 21 years of business at 45a Wood Street. However, our aims were not entirely mercenary. We catered for the needs of our canine customers by filling the RSPCA trough with fresh water each day. It was well patronised and much appreciated.

Being a small, friendly firm, Blackwell & Sons proved to be co-operative in executing special orders. I think the largest basket they ever made for us was for a Great Dane. It was like a big rectangular bedstead built on strong legs. One day a customer asked if we sold cushions for the baskets. Her pet was a Peke. That marked the beginning of another project. My mother and I started our own little business, making cushions to order. We had to buy the materials - mostly remnants; but the studs and saddle wool were purloined from the workshop!

To return to our basket trade, we soon added log baskets and bird tables to our stock. The dog baskets were put out on display every morning, but sometimes, if we were tired after a busy day, we would forget to take them in. The following morning, a friendly policeman would come into the shop, either carrying a couple of dog baskets, or advising us to pick them up from the police station, where they had spent the night.

Christmas trade was always exciting. As well as general sports equipment, we stocked all the latest board games, including the new popular Corinthian Bagatelle. My father drew the line at roulette - he was dead against gambling of any kind. This decision reflected his good Methodist upbringing.

Window-dressing competitions were a pleasure and challenge to our creative powers. I remember once entering a local competition. I was impressed by the fact that the natural rivalry that existed between the local shopkeepers did not prevent them from helping each other in their displays. We had decided to feature our extensive pigskin range. For the background of whole skins we needed for our window, we applied to our Walsall house, D Mason & Sons. They willingly co-operated. But the delightful camaraderie that existed among our fellow tradesmen encouraged us to look nearer home for other items needed to enhance the display.

Therefore, we had no hesitation in enlisting the help of our friend and business associate Stan Henson, the butcher, who provided a charming china pig for our centre-piece.

Miss Porker's small suitcase is, in fact, a pigskin jewel-case.

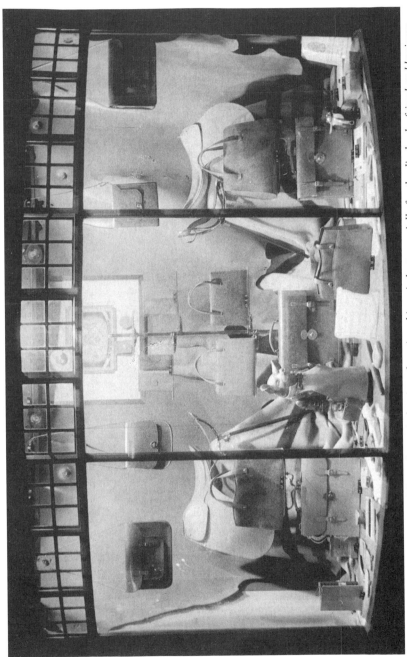

Standing proudly in the Wood Street bow window is a charming china pig lent especially for the display by friend and business associate Stan Henson, the butcher.

Father was a humble man - never known to stand on his dignity, and never expecting anyone to perform a task that he was not willing to undertake himself. I never ceased to wonder at his patience and humility. I remember one day having a very exacting customer. He wanted a cabin trunk. Finally, the deal was clinched. He handed the cheque to me, then turned, noticed my father standing there and ordered: "Bring the trunk to the car, my man!" With an inward chuckle, Father heaved up the trunk by the handle end and followed the young man. Ten minutes later he returned, still laughing. "And what's so funny about an able-bodied arrogant young fellow ordering the owner of the shop to carry his goods?" I snapped. Father quietly opened his hand "Well, he did give me a tip," he laughed, as he dropped the shiny sixpence into the charity box.

CHAPTER EIGHT

Kineton

We had a branch shop at Kineton. The property was owned by Frank Griffen, to whom a rent of ten shillings a week was paid. It was managed by Reg Tipping, who lived in the village. It was the smallest shop I had ever seen. Only a tidy man like Reg would have operated in so small a box space. The weekly takings were negligible, but the main purpose of the shop was to serve the Warwickshire Hunt. Their accounts were settled quarterly and dealt with at the Stratford office. Reg was a practical saddler and was well equipped to effect small repairs on the premises. The more complicated saddle work was brought to Stratford.

Southam Street, Kineton, where Thomas Beckett
rented a small branch shop.

Father went over to Kineton every Monday to collect work from the stables and to meet Reg's stock requirements. While doing business with Mr Gilson, the estate agent, Father never forgot the home front - part of which consisted of a clutch of hungry hens. So when he was offered cooked horse-meat from the kennels, he held his nose and accepted. The chickens were delighted - to them it was a feast most rich and rare.

Reg often accompanied Father to the Royal Show at Stoneleigh, where Becketts had a stand. (Our photograph shows them demonstrating their saddlery skills.)

Thomas Beckett (left) and Reg Tipping pictured on their regular stand at the Royal Show, Stoneleigh.

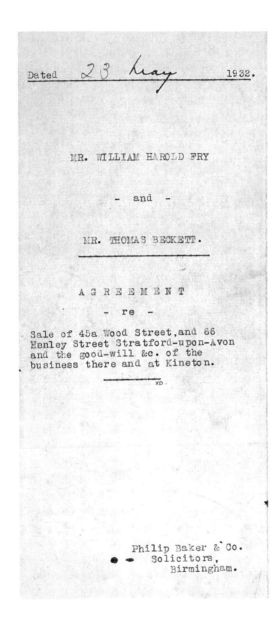

The agreement between William Harold Fry and Thomas Beckett
for the sale of the business at 45a Wood Street and 66 Henley Street
and the goodwill of the business there and at Kineton.

CHAPTER NINE

Our Country Plunges into War...

Things seemed to be going well in the world of commerce. Privately-owned shops in the tourist town of Stratford-upon-Avon prospered and Beckett's was no exception. By September 3, 1939 all this changed. Our country was plunged into war.

For the second time in their married life, Tom and Edith Beckett had to face the problems and restrictions of war conditions. The difference for them, this time, was that they were running their own business.

Tom's physical disability had exempted him from serving in the Forces in the 1914-18 War. This did not apply to his present family. He had no son, but the daughter, who was a product of the First World War, served in the Second. I was conscripted and joined up on 18 December, 1941.

The Beckett's home – Southville in Luddington Road, Stratford–upon–Avon.

My absence during the four years I served in the WAAF put pressure on our parents. Mother was, as ever, supportive. She took her part in keeping the business going over those difficult years. Living out of town, on Luddington Road, they made the daily journey to and from the shop on bicycles. The car spent most of its time in the garage.

Father had a petrol allowance for his preaching appointments. This was strictly reserved for the Sundays, when he was on the Lord's work conducting services in the village chapels in the Stratford Methodist circuit.

Father took his turn fire-watching. The fire-watchers' headquarters was in one of the offices in Central Chambers. He formed many friendships while serving with this gallant little team. I don't believe they ever had to cope with a fire on Father's duty period. However, it was a long night watch and the watchers gladly conversed and came to know each other, sitting drinking tea to keep themselves awake.

So once again, like the Grantham days, Mother spent some lonely evenings. True, she no longer had the squalling child as a doubtful companion. That child, me, was now serving in the Forces and my sister, Jean, was nursing at the Royal Masonic Hospital in London.

Over this period, most traders were struggling for survival. Beckett's catered chiefly for the luxury trade. Quality merchandise was in short supply. However, there were ways and means of occasionally obtaining small consignments of choice leather goods. Although the factories were committed to meeting War Office demands for supplies, some of the smaller Walsall houses managed to achieve a limited output of choice leather goods. Contrary to peace-time trading, when the wholesaler wooed the retailer for business, the war-time salesman was doing the customer a favour. For Beckett's, the one product that was in ready supply was the gas mask holder. Everyone was compelled to carry one, so it was big business.

On the Beckett home front, the large back garden at Southville, Luddington Road was subjected to a vigorous onslaught of the spade. Digging for victory was heavy work for Father and gardening was not his favourite pastime. But he was a true patriot and did not complain, especially when the vegetable crop was good.

When victory came, it was the flower garden that received the most attention. Like thousands of our fellow rejoicing countrymen, we planted in the front garden for all to behold our red geraniums, blue lobelia and white alyssum.

After the War, Beckett's branched out into camping equipment - tents, rucksacks, sleeping-bags, ground-sheets and all the accessories. One day we took our Welsh Collie down to the shop. Her name was Peggy abbreviated, of course, to Peg. She was very good and sat quietly at the back of the shop until a customer came in and asked for a dozen tent pegs.... up went her ears, and off she bounded, nearly knocking the young man down in her excitement. "What a friendly dog!" he exclaimed as he patted her silky head, failing to appreciate how his innocent request had excited her so much!

Edith and Thomas Beckett "digging for victory" in the garden of their home in Luddington Road.

Thomas Beckett in the garden of their Luddington Road home with their Welsh Collie, Peg.

The Mop was not a money-spinner for the local tradesmen. They certainly did not benefit from this disruptive fair. Then, as now, on 12 October the Mop took over the town. All roads were closed. Cables snaked treacherously across pavements. We had to barricade our windows to protect the plate glass. Business in the shops virtually came to a standstill. Was it worth opening at all? Well, for us, yes.

One annual customer we could not disappoint. He had a shooting gallery in Wood Street (not guns) and every year he came and replenished his stock of arrows and archery target faces at Beckett's.

Then half-an-hour before our usual closing time (5.30pm) two or three buxom fairground ladies came into the shop. They had spent their day collecting sixpences for a go on the Aunt Sally, coconut shy or magic wheel, handing over cheap prizes to the winners. Now they had come to Beckett's, asking to see some handbags. No salesmanship was needed on my part. As I opened the showcase, they seized upon the largest, most expensive quality models. No fuss. They knew what they wanted. They paid up cheerfully, handing over wads of bank notes from which exuded a strange aroma, a kind of mixture of hot dogs, garlic and cheap scent.

We did not complain. It was all 'grist to the till', to misquote the well-known saying, on a day when the little wooden box could have found itself somewhat hungry!

A war-time picture of the Beckett family. The author is on the left of the picture, with her sister, Jean between her mother and father.

CHAPTER TEN

The Famous Riding Saddle

Eddie Ling was a friend and business associate. His London-based saddlery firm produced beautiful hide shoulder bags (Ling's Slings) as well as catering for the riding fraternity.

We looked forward to his visits, when he called to show us Ling's latest designs, and collect the order. He was a great story-teller and would frequently enliven the proceedings with entertaining anecdotes.

His two children, Patsy and Richard, often featured in these stories. During one of our buying sessions, we were most impressed when he told us that the Trade Association had commissioned Lings to make a pony saddle for the young Prince Charles. It was a gift. Then, with great glee, Eddie recorded that the night before it was due to be delivered, two bare-bottomed little Lings had sneaked into the saddle-room and, in turn, solemnly occupied the royal seat.

*A pony saddle made by Lings which was similar to the one especially made for Prince Charles. The saddles seemed to be a popular resting place for **bear** bottoms...*

By 1952, after 20 years of successful trading, we were well and truly established in Stratford-upon-Avon. It was gratifying to know that we had earned a reputation for good service. We enjoyed pleasant relationships with our wholesale firms and our valued customers. It was a most satisfactory state of affairs. We were not unduly concerned that our lease was due to expire the following year.

However, when we applied for a new lease, we had a shock coming. Our landlady was unwilling to grant it. Our little business was threatened.

Being offered only an annual tenancy, after 21 years of successful trading in a going concern, gave no cause for celebration. Hence, our coming-of-age the following year posed a great worry. It was not a comfortable situation.

The question that stared us in the face was 'Where do we go from here?'

PEAK THREE

CHAPTER ELEVEN

The Threat

When Bailey's, the greengrocer's, came on to the market, it was the home of the well-known Bailey family who had traded and lived above the shop for many years. It was the first freehold property put up for sale in Stratford-upon-Avon this century. It would need to be partially demolished and rebuilt to meet the needs of Beckett's business.

However, the site was ideal. Not only was it central, it was a mere 30 yards from the present premises and on the same side of the street!

The auction of the property was scheduled to take place at the Town Hall on Wednesday 7 May, 1951. Our main concern was financial. Up to what figure would our parents dare to bid? Of course, if any of the big companies had their eyes on it, we would not stand a chance.

Mercifully, we did not learn until later that offers of £10,000 had been made before the auction. So how much could the family safely raise to buy this property that was becoming increasingly desirable? At last the great day arrived. Mr and Mrs Beckett approached the Town Hall with some trepidation and not a little faith that this impossible dream of personal ownership of a business and property might come true.

That memorable afternoon, customers at 45a Wood Street did not receive the usual patient, undivided attention they expected. The assistant and I hustled them off as quickly as possible, so that we could rush to the shop door to meet our parents, whose news was so eagerly awaited.

As we reached the door for the twentieth time, a fellow tradesman shouted from across the street

"They've bought it!" We just hugged each other. It was indeed a wonderful moment.

Bailey's fruit and vegetable shop at 43 Wood Street before it became the new home for Thomas Beckett's thriving business.

Ten minutes later a jubilant Mr and Mrs Beckett confirmed the great news. They had bought the property for £8,750.

Once the initial excitement of purchasing the property had worn off a little, we had to get down to the serious business of raising the money. We all four contributed. Even our modest Post Office savings were poured into the great venture. For the dream to become reality, professionals had to be employed. We appointed Edwin H Earp Badger to be our architects. They immediately began to negotiate with the Regional Licensing Officer of the Ministry of Works to obtain the building licence. At first we were wholeheartedly supported by the Town Council. However, when Mr Badger's plans were submitted, objections were raised.

It was a question of the infringement of the Right of Light. The Land and Building Committee was not satisfied with the proposed design of the upper storey overlooking Cooks Alley. After much discussion, we reluctantly agreed to put dormer windows in the offices above the shop. In their letter of 14 November, the Ministry of Works stated that while they were prepared to give favourable consideration to the issuing of the building licence, it was understood that putting the remaining buildings in a state of repair was Mr Beckett's responsibility. Mr Badger's cryptic reply was "that the said buildings are of no possible use to our client, or anyone else". The matter was quietly dropped.

On 19 December, 1952 Mr King of Evesham was appointed to prepare a Bill of Quantities. On 27 February, 1953 tenders were sent out to builders. Mr Badger was duly able to inform the Regional Licensing Officer that the successful contender for Beckett's building scheme was the Avon Building Company, Wellesbourne. The amount required to be licensed was £5,400 plus £550 for interior shopfittings.

As far back as 14 November, our local MP, John Profumo, had negotiated with the Regional Licensing Officer, and given his support to the immediate issue of a building licence. The months went by, and no progress was made. In desperation, we found we had to appeal to our caring MP again and again, when the bureaucratic machine seemed to have come to a standstill. Then, on 16 March, two letters were written, the contents of which were to brighten our hitherto gloomy horizon. The one letter from Mr Badger to John Profumo's agent, Mr Bond, outlined the latest details of our building project. He concluded: "Once more, we shall be most grateful to have the assistance of John Profumo and your good self in obtaining an immediate issue of a building licence for this scheme".

The letter from the Regional Licensing Office informed Mr Badger that the coveted, long-awaited licence was granted. Then a letter from the House of Commons dated 20 March, 1953 confirmed our belief that the necessary pressure to achieve the satisfactory result had been applied by our MP.

The months dragged on. Still it was all on paper, but nothing more. Action at last! The bulldozers came in. The dust began to fly. Prince Philip's birthday (10 June) was celebrated at 43 Wood Street by the vomiting forth of the last and largest consignment of rubble. Barrow-loads were trundled from the site through the alley and duly tipped on the Henley Street pavement where a lorry was drawn up to cart the rubbish away. The mound consisted of small boulders, slabs, plaster, odd lengths of fuse wire and large quantities of rose-coloured dust. It impeded the progress of the unfortunate pedestrians who were compelled to pick their way through or around it. The old property was not exactly demolished. It was rather scooped-out. The walls and original shop ceiling were knocked down, but the upper ceiling, roofing and quaint little garret on the top were retained. Over the next few weeks, progress was made, but weaknesses in the structure were revealed.

Walls that had not been pulled down by the builders collapsed of

71

their own accord when neighbouring bricks were disturbed. Floors and wooden partitions no longer concealed from view by flaking plaster, grime and cobwebs, told the sorry tale of death by the silent enemy, dry rot.

When the discovery was made, one of the builders approached my father with a confidential "Would you please come along to the site, Mr Beckett?" The advice given was: "It will be cheaper in the long run to remove this bad patch, and replace it with new material. It will only cost another £20." This little ritual was repeated with startling regularity and the extra charges mentioned so casually gradually mounted up. It was rather late in the day to declare wisely: "It would have been better to have blasted it to the ground and started afresh."

However, the cost incurred for total demolition and rebuilding would certainly have exceeded the figure (£5,400) submitted to the licensing office on 16 March. He could have delayed the granting of the licence, or even rejected the scheme altogether. In spite of the setbacks, the building began to take shape. The Beckett's corner of our dreams began to assume the character of the architect's sketches that had filled us with wonder when we had gazed proudly and unbelievably upon them, so many months ago. At the auction, our parents had bought the property with all the faith and reckless assurance of visionaries. We had never seriously doubted the wisdom of that afternoon's work, but there had been grey periods of apprehension.

Perhaps the most ingenious description of the transformation that was taking place at 43 Wood Street came from the architect's seven-year-old daughter. She explained "My Daddy made the pictures for this shop. He made a big hole, but the builders filled it in. My Daddy gave them the paper to show them how to do it."

The lady who suffered the greatest inconvenience from the demolition was Mrs Crowhurst, who lived at Pan's Cottage, next to the site. Day after day the dust seeped into her little front room and beyond. She was most tolerant, and even admitted that she enjoyed watching the work in progress. However, when I came by the site on my way home one evening, I saw this good lady standing outside her cottage door crouching over her broom. She gently swept the dust away from her front door, stroked it into a little pile, collected it up in a dustpan, then with a delightful touch of defiance, threw it back into the builder's yard from whence it came!

I should mention at this point that on 9 June, the company T. Beckett (Saddler) Limited was formed. It was the first directors' meeting and the directors - all four of them - were there in full force. There was my father and mother, my sister Jean, and myself.

No. C. 173.

No. 510138

Certificate of Incorporation

I Hereby Certify, That

T. BECKETT (SADDLER) LIMITED

is this day Incorporated under the Companies Act, 1948, and that the Company is **Limited**.

Given under my hand at London this .... Twenty-eighth .... day of .... July .... One Thousand Nine Hundred and Fifty -two.

A. I. Ruby

Registrar of Companies

Wt. 18384/3681 11m 7/51 F.M.&S. 51-8103

The Certificate of Incorporation announcing the fact that T. Beckett (Saddler) was now a Limited company.

T. BECKETT (SADDLER) LIMITED

MINUTES OF THE FIRST MEETING OF DIRECTORS HELD AT WOOD STREET, STRATFORD-ON-AVON ON 1ST AUGUST, 1952.

Present:- T. Beckett (in the Chair)
Edith Elizabeth Beckett
Constance Mary Beckett.

In attendance:- R. W. Hobbs
J. G. White

Registration

Mr. White reported the registration of the Company and produced the statutory books. The company's seal was produced and it was resolved that the seal as impressed be formally adopted.

Directors.

The directors named in the Articles of Association namely:-

Thomas Beckett,
Edith Elizabeth Beckett,
Constance Mary Beckett,
Jean Christine Beckett

were formally appointed.

Chairman

It was resolved that Mr. Thomas Beckett be appointed Chairman.

Secretary

It was resolved that Constance Mary Beckett be appointed Secretary.

Bankers

It was resolved that Barclays Bank Ltd., be appointed Bankers of the Company.

That the said Bank be and they are hereby authorised:-

1. To honour and comply with all Cheques, Draft Bills, Promissory Notes, Acceptances negotiable instruments and orders expressed to be drawn accepted made or given on behalf of this Company at any time or times whether the banking account or accounts of this Company are overdrawn by any payment thereof or in relation thereto or are in credit or otherwise.

2. To honour and comply with all instructions to deliver or dispose of any securities or documents or property held by the Bank on behalf of the Company

Provided any such Cheques, Draft Bills, Promissory Notes, Acceptances negotiable instruments order and instructions are signed by Thomas Beckett or Constance Mary Beckett.

—contd—

Minutes of the first meeting of the Directors of T. Beckett (Saddler) Limited.

CHAPTER TWELVE

The Green Monster

Our worst bogey was the telephone cabinet situated in Cooks Alley. Its position against a blank wall was quite acceptable, not inconveniencing anyone; but its position in the centre of the frontage that was to be occupied by our third box window was unthinkable. Hence, on our behalf, the architect wrote to the GPO* at Coventry to advise them of our building scheme and that it was necessary to remove the obstacle at the earliest possible date. This letter of 13 May 1952 pointed out that the cabinet must go, at the very latest, before building operations began. Well, for the next 13 months all went quiet on the Coventry front. Over this period our letters and phone calls were ignored or simply not dealt with.

We were desperate. The "monster" was still there. No sign of its removal. So once again we had to appeal to our caring MP John Profumo, through his agent, Mr Bond, who I telephoned. He was surprised there had been no action. "Could you possibly hurry things up?" I pleaded.

His genial reply was "I shall be phoning Johnnie later. I'll mention it. I know his secretary has written to Coventry. I'll try and find out what's happening."

I thanked him, then went along to the site just in case the wretched obstacle had miraculously disappeared. Of course, it hadn't. Gupwell's men (shopfitters) were on site putting the finishing touches to the window frames. One man was standing on some tall steps near the area where the third box window in the alley would be. "Have you got something heavy I can drop on that thing?" I called, indicating my pet aversion. "Two men came and looked at it yesterday morning," he told me. "That's all they do - look at it!" I retorted. He laughed and continued "Well, they measured it

* *The General Post Office was originally responsible for telephones and dark green was its corporate colour.*

75

up and put something down in a little book."

"Oh, did they?" I was still dubious, not allowing myself to become too hopeful at this stage. Sensing my doubts he added encouragingly "They were two officials." Then he swivelled round on his perch and pointed across the road. "They went over there."

So, at last, they had reached the talking stage.

John Profumo pictured in 1953 when he was
Thomas Beckett's Member of Parliament.

On 11 July 1953, I unlocked the shop door at 45a, gathered up the post and ran through it. Only one sealed letter bearing a 2¹/₂d. stamp. I turned it over, saw the House of Commons seal on the back, dropped the rest of the mail on the floor and slit open the envelope. My heart missed a beat as I quickly scanned the single typed sheet signed by John Profumo's secretary.

"I understand that work on the removal of the box is going to begin on Monday and its transfer to another place will be completed within a few days."

A few days! I was trembling with excitement as I rushed to the phone and dialled my home number. I read the letter out to my mother. Her practical answer to her doubting Thomas daughter was "I told you it would be all right".

From: John Profumo, OBE., MP.

20th March 1953.

Dear Mr. Beckett,

You will by now probably have been informed that the licence has been granted for the alterations at 43 Wood Street.

I am very glad to have been able to be of assistance to you in this matter, and I look forward to seeing your new premises when the work has been completed.

With my kindest regards.

Yours sincerely,

[signature]

T. Beckett, Esq.,
45a Wood Street,
Stratford-on-Avon.

One of a number of letters sent to Thomas Beckett by John Profumo in relation to the move from 45a to 43 Wood Street.

It was Monday morning 12 July at 9am. On my way to opening up 45a I glanced up the alley. As ever, the "monster" stood there looking so solid and so permanent. No telephone van in sight. We had a busy morning at 45a. I coped with the customers, but my mind was in Cooks Alley.

From: Secretary to John Profumo, OBE., MP.

10th July 1953.

Dear Mr. Beckett,

Mr. Profumo is away today on a speaking tour up in Lancashire, and as soon as I heard from Mr. Bond this morning that your problem, which Mr. Profumo has already taken up with the authorities, has not yet been resolved and that work on your premises is at a standstill, I rang up the Telephone Manager at Coventry to find out the position.

I understand that work on the removal of the box is going to begin on Monday, and its transfer to another place will be completed within a few days. I will, of course, tell Mr. Profumo this news on his return.

Yours sincerely,

Rosemary Money

T. Beckett, Esq.,
45a Wood Street,
Stratford-on-Avon.

The letter from Mr Profumo's secretary, Rosemary Money, which signalled that action was at last to be taken to remove that awful green monster.

As soon as I was free, I ran along to the site. I spoke to my merry friend, who had taken up his favourite position perched on the steps. "It's still there, I see. Has anyone been?" "Oh yes, two of them," he grinned. "Now they've gone off somewhere." "Oh," I sighed, "why on earth don't they get started?" "They came about 10 o'clock," he told me. "They said 'Do you want this moving?' 'Yes, and jolly quick, or I'll drop something heavy on it,' I told them."

How he enjoyed baiting those poor telephone men! "Did they say where they're going to put it?" I asked. "Yes," he reported solemnly, "in the middle of the shop."

Real progress at last. The "monster" was no longer just an object of observation; the process of removal had begun. I was fascinated by the little tent the men erected over the pavement to protect them from the elements while they were working. The sound of the voices of the two men in blue overalls, issuing from the shelter, was music to my ears. I am ashamed to admit that the sight of the green telephone van, adding to the traffic congestion in Wood Street, filled me with joy.

There was little progress that day. Complications were indicated when the two workmen sat in their shelter awaiting instructions, while three officials stood conferring outside the tent. It was about 4 o'clock.

Ten minutes later, the three officials walked to the end of the alley, where they stopped and talked again. At 4.30pm they all vanished - workmen, officials and the transport. So much for that day's work! Workmen appeared about 10am and left at 4.30pm. They still seemed to be occupied with counting leads, checking numbers, erecting the tent in the morning, taking it down at night, covering up the hole and departing.

We received a delegation from the telephone people to discuss the removal and future home of the terrible cabinet. Permission from the Town Council was needed. "Who pays?" I murmured, when I overheard figures of £500 and £600 mentioned. "Oh, the department pays," I was reassured.

Gupwell's men had become as obsessed as I was about the "green monster", so I was not surprised when I visited the site to be greeted with a gleeful "It's dead. All the wires have been removed. Doesn't matter what you do to a corpse."

Apparently the Leamington men had finished their job. The final actual removal involved ripping up half the pavement and would be executed by an expert from London.

I was working at 45a when Father walked into the shop and announced quaintly "I've just come from the funeral." I eyed him quizzically, then tumbled to his meaning. "You don't mean - oh, has it really gone?" I didn't wait for permission. I ran along the pavement, pushed open the corrugated door of the hoarding and, sure enough, found five men crouching over a space. The ugly "green monster" had gone, but its fangs, deep in the ground, still had to be drawn. Four men watched while the fifth man worked the quivering drill. The sparks flew as this final operation took place.

The removal operation caused chaos in the alley. Poor old Cooks Alley was wounded by pickaxes tearing up her surface slabs and cutting into her entrails. There was a huge hole under Father's office window. Bricks were piled high where the hated cabinet had stood in front of the third box window. The alley was receiving a gash in a fresh place to make way for the atrocity to be regrafted. No, we did not lose our "green monster".

The cabinet's new home was only a couple of yards away under the office window. It looked smaller than its predecessor. Perhaps it was the new silver colour that gave this impression. It no longer offended me.

As a point of interest, the cabinet was not disturbed again until 1984 (five years after Beckett's had ceased trading) when a new, wider cabinet replaced our troublesome friend.

CHAPTER THIRTEEN

Settling In

I found myself standing in the middle of what would be the new shop. I had to stand because it was impossible to move around without running into manifold objects covering the floor area. Lengths of wood for the new cupboards were placed along the wall in front of the box window spaces. There were bicycles propped against the shiny new fittings; odd shapes of wood bearing our name, with measurements chalked on them; a wooden form cluttered with shopfitters' tools, and a well-worn plan of the shop. On the floor was a box containing two silver cylinders that proved on closer examination to be rolls of sheet zinc. In the midst of all this was an upturned wheelbarrow on a pile of gravel and shavings.

Although I could hear the workmen busy behind the hoarding and the sound of Friday shoppers walking through the alley penetrated my ears, I felt quite alone in a world of my own. I had a vision of myself working in this space, spending God knows how many years of my life serving the public, building up a business that already had excellent foundations, selling quality merchandise - and I was afraid. It was not the earlier fear, born of long months of frustration, when the building stood dull, dirty, untouched before the granting of the building licence. It was a new fear, subtle and treacherous, a bright glittering fear, a fear of the very thing I had desired so desperately.

It was the blind panic of success, of being harnessed to my god of commerce, unable to break away, not wanting to break away, a slave to my own ambition. I wanted it and hoped for it when it seemed so far away. I was filled with joy and pride every time we seemed to come a little closer to the fulfilment of the dream. Ah well! We should see. I shook myself free of these thoughts and stepped out into the sunshine.

On another occasion I found myself having a real touch of nostalgia for the old shop. I was working at the new shop one evening when I discovered I needed something I had left at 45a. It was growing dusk. I went in, switched on the light and locked the door behind me. I looked around. The place had a desolate air. Robbed of the last stock that had been transferred to the other shop, it looked unhappy, tired and unloved. I felt a sudden pang at the thought of leaving it.

The new shop had possessed me so completely there was no place left in my heart to mourn leaving 45a. Now its shabby, silent and some-how peaceful friendliness and familiarity was comforting.

We had hoped to open in time for the Coronation of Queen Elizabeth II, but it was now evident that it would be several more weeks before the shopfitters completed their task. While my parents urged them to move a little faster, I did not, for once, share their sense of urgency. I enjoyed my daily pilgrimage to the site so much that I did not altogether relish the thought of completion. Surely nothing - even the proud moment of ultimate possession - could surpass the daily ripple of excitement I had experienced over the past few months. Every time I visited the site, there was something new to wonder at. I had not outgrown my childish delight in anticipation. The new shop was still something of a surprise packet. I was loathe to rush at it, enjoying the gradual revelation.

* * *

My parents and I were told that the plate-glass had arrived and that the shop windows would be in by mid-day. Excited at the prospect of seeing the new windows fitted, we went along to the site at the appointed hour.

As we entered the shop my eye was immediately drawn to the little window, my bonus display unit for wallets and small leather goods. It looked all askew. On closer investigation, I discovered that there was at least a half-inch discrepancy between the wall and the window. Tom, Gupwell's foreman, expected us to be pleased with the four main windows and we were. They looked splendid, but that half-inch off true in my small window by the door I could not and would not live with. The smug expression on Tom's face faded when I drew his attention to the fault. "It's the wall that's out of true," he declared, "not my measurements. They're checked with a spirit level."

He was ruffled. A glance from Father cautioned me to drop the subject until Mr Moore, the supervisor, arrived. When he entered the shop, I quietly piloted him back to the offensive window and pointed out the fault. The poor man was not his usual debonair self. He had been to the dentist and was nursing a swollen mouth. He said nothing, just frowned and shook his head. "Do you think it's right?" I queried tentatively. "N-no," he muttered.

Gaining confidence at this admission I went on "Do you consider it a good advertisement for your firm?" "No, I don't," he conceded. "I'll see about it."

We stayed discreetly out of earshot while he went back into the shop to reprimand Tom. After a few minutes he returned. He looked most unhappy. "The whole window will have to come out!"

He spoke very quietly as if he was afraid he had offended Tom, who obviously resented having to do his work all over again. I carefully avoided Tom when he came out with his screwdriver and started taking the window apart. I was very sorry about the whole affair, but also glad and relieved that it had been put right before it was too late.

* * *

I was somewhat shattered at the appearance of the shop when the hoarding was removed. The new exposed building was a real mess. It just looked like something that was not there before. The windows were smeared white inside, but through the flimsy film over the first box window in the alley, I espied Tom and his pal sitting munching substantial sandwiches. A barrow stood in front of the second box window. I watched a small boy scooping up handfuls of sand from a pile heaped at the entrance of the shop. At that stage the only indication of the ownership of the shop was the brass plate above the letter-box. The T. Beckett letters had yet to be fixed above the windows.

The Antler sign had been removed from above the old shop and now hung proudly over the fine, imposing corner of the new block. He seemed to be looking down as if he knew that the Antler display unit would soon be coming through the door below. Denis Rowe, of Antler, had telephoned to tell us that the unit would only cost us £25. The £60 cost of installation would be borne by Antler.

But when Mr Badger called in to see Father, he greeted him rather surprisingly with the words: "You're breaking the law!" My father blinked. He was one of the most law-abiding citizens I have ever known. "That sign," Mr Badger went on severely. "Not the Antler," I broke in.

"It's against the law. You should have asked permission first." "Who on earth from?" my father asked. "The Town Council." "But it's always hung over the shop. It's only been moved a few yards along the street."

My father was a patient man, but this did annoy him. It seemed so petty. The poor old Antler sign was the centre of discussion for the rest of the morning. We had a word with our fellow Councillor Eric Baildham, who promised to speak up for us at the next Council meeting.

Mr Badger got on the phone to Mr Smart, the Borough Surveyor, and between them they decided that it would be diplomatic to take the sign down until permission was granted. Then Mr Badger proceeded to make a list of particulars concerning the size, colour when illuminated and distance from the ground when suspended to submit to the next Council meeting. Permission was ultimately granted.

CHAPTER FOURTEEN

The Floor

The shop floor area was screeded in preparation for the laying of the blocks. I was working at 45 when Tom came along from the site. He looked so serious I teased "You do look sombre, what's wrong?"

He lowered his voice to a conspiratorial whisper "I don't want to interfere, but ....."

"What now?" I thought with a sinking heart. "The floor blocks. They've come. But they're no good at all. It will spoil the whole job. They're too thin, only 3/8in. I'd come and look at them if I were you." Then he added: "Don't mention I told you." "Thanks Tom, I'll come along right away."

When I arrived on the site, Tom was busy fixing the gilt letters (T. Beckett) on the facia of the large Wood Street window. As I entered, he pointed down just inside the door. There they were, a pathetic little stack of lightweight, fragile-looking, biscuit-thin slices, more like a child's toy pack than a set of blocks suitable for covering a place of business where thousands (we hoped) of feet would tread over many years.

As I examined one of these wafers, Gerald Parsons appeared in the doorway. I handed the specimen over to him. "What do you think of them?" "I don't like them," came the prompt reply. "They won't last five minutes. This floor is screeded for $3/4$in blocks." I reported to Father who got on the phone to Mr Badger. The outcome of all this was that while Mr Badger and Mr Stowe agreed that the blocks were wrong, neither would accept responsibility for placing the order.

Mr Stowe agreed that there had been a mistake. He was eloquent on the subject of the inadequacy of the blocks for our purpose. He quoted a case in which this type of block had been laid only nine months ago.

They had worn so badly, the floor had to be taken up and re-laid. When Mr Badger phoned Father, he murmured "Don't mention it to Mr Stowe, but he ordered the blocks that thickness months ago." However, something had to be done, whoever was at fault.

The following day, Hewitson's representative turned up with samples of the new blocks. Father, Mr Badger and I trooped along to the new shop and the salesmen placed the blocks on the rough surface for our inspection. They looked good. They were solid and the colours ranged from a pale sepia to dark brown. I had no hesitation in making my choice. It was a beautiful honey-coloured block, with a finely-grained surface. To my tentative enquiry: "How much extra will this add to the original quotation?" I was told £38. I was by now immune to shocks where extra payments were concerned.

I did not exclaim as I would have done six or even three months previously. I just gulped and kept quiet. The vote was unanimous. The colour and quality of the selected block seemed quite perfect to me. I couldn't wait to see it as a complete covering for our floor.

But I had to wait. A week later the work began. The actual laying of the floor took only a few days. It was a work of art. The young craftsman knelt at the top of the shop, starting at the left-hand side. He lifted a block from the main stack, dipped it in a pot of tar by his side, planted it, then gave it a neat tap with a little hammer. The next block received the same treatment, then it was clapped tight against its neighbour. With clockwork precision he glided from side to side. The rhythmic exercise continued as the golden blocks merged and seemed to flow smoothly, gradually spreading until, like an incoming tide, the whole surface was transformed into a beautiful, smooth golden quality floor. The following day, the lad returned to fit in all the awkward shapes around the edge.

The final polishing was supervised by Hewitson's manager. For two days the area was out of bounds. Then came the great moment, when we were allowed to walk on the new floor. I was so overawed by the sheer beauty of the surface I scarcely dare step over the threshold. It was holy ground to me. The young craftsman whose skill in laying the floor had impressed me so much was a lad of few words. When I exclaimed rather effusively "It's magnificent," his quiet response was "Glad you like it".

But later, just before he left, having completed the job, he talked to Father and confessed proudly that it was the best job he had done for a long time. Evidently, his firm agreed. He received a bonus of £3.

As there were still odd jobs for the builders to complete in the shop, it was necessary for Mr Stowe and his two men to have access to the 'holy ground'. Hence sawdust was scattered over the shining surface to protect it from being marked by scraping ladders and tins containing paint, not to mention boots of workmen tramping about. They had their job to do, so understandably they did not share our reverence for the floor. Now it looked more like a circus ring than a ballroom floor. When the Antler stand was delivered, Gerald made way for it by sweeping the sawdust away. I jokingly suggested that we opened the shop with a tea dance. "But leave a bit of sawdust in the corner for Mr Stowe's men, or they'll ruin the floor!" I said rather unkindly looking straight at Mr Stowe's nephew, Fred, the chief offender.

"What a name you've got, Fred," someone teased.

He looked crestfallen. "Don't come to the dance in your hob-nailed boots," Gerald added wickedly. I winced at the very thought of hob-nailed boots. Poor Fred! He must have hated that floor.

Fred Stowe, known to his mates as "Stowey" was nephew and employee of Mr Stowe, our builder. Interestingly, he had worked on this site before. Thirty years earlier, at the tender age of ten, he had been employed by Mr Bailey as an errand boy. In those days Baileys imported green bananas from the Canaries and ripened them in the cellar at 43 Wood Street. They were then packed in long boxes and delivered around the town in a green van. However, when the branch shops in Sheep Street and High Street needed restocking, errand boy Fred was sent trundling off with replenishments on his carrier bike. He was paid half a crown (2s. 6d.) a week.

We were so proud of our beautiful parquet floor, we were quite fanatical about maintaining its lovely golden surface. Later, when we started trading, I would stay on after the shop was closed to wax polish and hand-bumper. It was good exercise, but somewhat tiring. As a point of interest, when we ceased trading in September, 1979, we 'lost' the floor for ever. One of the first things our first tenant (Rodney Webb Sports Shop) did was to fit a carpet. Subsequent tenants had the same idea. Our pride and joy now languishes under a carpet hidden by the latest tenant - the AA - from the light of day!

CHAPTER FIFTEEN

Betwixt Two Shops

The telephone engineers were still working in the alley. The front shop entrance and the side door leading into the passage at the back were virtually blocked with piles of rubble. A small temporary tent was erected in the alley in front of the shop door. On reaching this spot, I felt a blow-lamp about my ankles. I peered through the flap of the tent and a grimy face appeared. "How long will it take?" I enquired doubtfully. "We shall be finished tonight." Back he went.

"We need to get through with goods from the other shop and we're expecting deliveries," I persisted. The face came out again "Oh, that's all right," he said cheerfully, and disappeared.

We had earlier received a call from the railway station to say that they had three crates of goods for us. Where would we like them delivered? The answer was: "To the new shop."

Later that afternoon, we set out to deal with these goods that had to be unpacked, checked and marked off. The problem was to find a space to work in. The stockroom was dusty and cluttered with builder's tools. Arthur's workshop and bench seemed to be a sort of workman's cloakroom - a place for overalls, caps, steps and tins of distemper. Fred Stowe was still in the shop with his ladder and tins of stain and brushes.

Hewitson's man was putting the finishing touches to the floor. The general explanation from all departments was: "We're just finishing something off." We managed to complete our task somehow, but it was wearing.

* * *

I tried to discipline myself to shut 43 Wood Street out of my mind when I locked the shop door at night. However, when I went to bed and tried to sleep I was not strong-willed enough to check my clamouring thoughts. They crowded in. As I tossed and turned, I mentally placed handbags, despatch cases and trinket boxes in my new windows. I rearranged shelves and fittings a dozen different ways. Even when sleep claimed me, the handbags and suitcases crept into my dreams so that when I awoke, there seemed to be no difference between night and morning. I was not tired, only excited and eager to be at it again.

That evening I put in my usual voluntary overtime and set about dressing the new shop windows. Dressing the big window for the first time was quite a challenge. It was so different in shape, particularly the height, from the bow window at 45a. It needed a different display technique that I had to discover. I spent the whole evening experimenting with this area that was as yet unfamiliar to me. I had dressed it in my imagination in the twilight hours between sleep and waking so many, many times. Now this was it for real. I took off my sandals, put on some soft slippers and stepped up into the window.

My first job was the practical one of scraping away the tiny spots of whitewash that still stuck to the glass; then I stood and cleaned the leaded lights at the top of the window. My final task before starting the real job was polishing the base. I got up too quickly to step out of the window and bumped my head. I had a lot to learn. I was happy when the creative part began. I had reserved a suite of London tan orient fibre luggage to grace the corner. They were handsome cases and pleased my eye displayed in this way. From there I experimented, placing and rearranging sports equipment to balance the luggage and leather goods. I was quite satisfied with the result of my labours, not because I had mastered the window, but because I had tested and got the feel of it. I knew more or less what I wanted from it, and what I could do with it.

* * *

The help, encouragement and advice we received from our business associates was heart-warming. Cliff Millington, from the butcher's shop over the road, devoted a whole evening of his time to carrying all the suitcases from our old shop to the new one. He lined the cases up for me while I placed them on the shelves we had designed for the purpose.

Hence, half the long side wall was literally lined with suitcases. Next to this unit was the Antler stand, on permanent loan from the firm.

The famous 'Boots unit' occupied the rest of this wall space, opposite the front shop door.

When I protested to Cliff that he was working too hard, he retorted "Don't be daft, that's what I came for."

Then, for good measure, he got down on his knees, cleaned the inside of the top counter case, and fixed the glass shelves.

* * *

We did not buy any new shop furniture. It was all either transferred from 45a or bought secondhand. The 'Boots' mahogany showcase had to be sawn in half to fit into the new shop area. One half went to the top of the shop, next to the office door; and the other half was placed on the wall side opposite the shop door. The glass counter showcase was transferred from the old shop, but we needed two more counters to cover the larger area.

When Burtons, the tailors, moved to their new premises, the manager offered us two counters they wanted to dispose of. We accepted, with alacrity. The useful, shallow counter drawers that had displayed men's ties, men's handkerchiefs and cravats, would now be filled with small leather goods, jewel cases, stud boxes and brandy flasks. The three counters were spaced diagonally across the shop.

When Gupwell's sales manager tried to sell us some chromium-plated display stands I demurred when I saw the price. Even when he offered a 10 per cent discount I was not enthusiastic. He left the list with us. No order followed. I don't know whether they thought us thrifty or just plain mean. I even made my own price tickets. Later, we did invest in a set of plastic tickets. That was luxury, indeed.

Another of our eccentricities was our refusal to buy a cash register. Our little old-fashioned till, that had to be fed with a paper cash roll, served us to the end.

Mother solved one of my window-dressing problems when she bought a long, narrow, 6in high form, from Baileys sale yard. I used it to elevate my hockey stick stand (designed and made by Gerald Parsons) in the centre of the big window. An application of lavender polish improved its appearance wonderfully. Yet another sale bargain!

* * *

91

The distance between 45a and 43 Wood Street was so short that stock could be transferred along the pavement. Our final exodus of stock removal took place on Thursday 10 September, 1953 ready for the opening of the new shop the following day.

Another of the Beckett's eccentricities was that they refused to buy a new cash register for the new Wood Street shop. Their little old–fashioned till, that had to be fed with a paper cash roll, was to last them from the moment they opened for business in Bridge Street, Thetford in 1920 until they eventually put up the shutters for good at 43 Wood Street, Stratford–upon–Avon in 1979!

There were a few hockey sticks still on display in the window of the old shop. On one of my journeys between the two, Wendy Lovell, a friend of mine, stopped me and asked if she could buy the Blue Flash hockey stick in the window. "Of course, no trouble," I assured her. One thing less to carry to number 43.

So this one item on the till meant that we did not lose even a half day's business!

CHAPTER SIXTEEN

The Great Day

The dream came true. Not a great deal of business was transacted on that first wonderful day in the new shop. People stepped in or just popped their heads round the door out of curiosity. A friendly policeman called from the doorway: "Your new shop is the talk of the town. I keep hearing folk say 'Have you seen Beckett's?' ".

The comments were, in fact, as varied as the people who made them. They were mostly complimentary. The charming Mrs Fordham Flower (now Lady Flower) floated in, then stood still. Her eyes swept over the whole area of the shop. Then she beamed "How perfectly lovely. You must be enchanted".

Our near neighbour and business associate Mrs Jackson (Eugenes) came to wish us well. She was particularly interested in the lighting. Much careful thought had been put into the blending of colour in the egg-crate fittings. We had settled for a mix of warm white and pink tubes to shed the kindest possible light on our leather goods, especially the pigskin. Mrs Jackson told us that she had a similar problem of avoiding distortion of colours of fabrics under artificial light. We were only too happy for her to bring along some of the gowns to test them under our lighting.

Mr Wilson (Esquires) popped in to congratulate us. "This is really magnificent," he remarked.

Then he looked down and laughed "You've got my floor!" The lighting, the parquet floor, even the angle of the counters were enthusiastically approved. The postman's comment was: "Lovely place you've got here now."

One of my first customers was a good-looking young man who

bought a note-case. After he had paid for it he stood for a moment, gazed around, then murmured "It's a palace!" and wandered out.

Our customers who belonged to the riding and hunting fraternity were not quite so enthusiastic. On that first day, the shop did rather give the impression of being basically a travel, leather goods and sports shop, rather than a saddler's. Mr Rodocanachi implied his preference for the old shop, when he said politely: "You do look fashionable."

The shopfront and (below) the interior of the new shop
at 43 Wood Street, Stratford–upon–Avon.

Mr Dronsfield spelt out the objection: "Where's the saddlery department?"

Mrs Gaskell shared these sentiments, but she expressed her disapproval more vociferously

"What have you done with the saddlery?" "Give us a chance," I said in a tiny voice. "It is only our first day."

Still, I realised that there was much organising of stock and display to think about before the needs of all our customers were satisfactorily met. I remembered that just before we left 45a, David Marland had teasingly threatened: "I shall never be comfortable bringing my harness repairs into that shop. You'll be far too grand to sell anything but handbags at yonder wonderful emporium." I assured him that the saddlery side of the business would not be neglected. "I shall be too awed to step inside the door," he mocked as he departed. Fortunately, Mr Marland did not desert us.

On the whole, people were extremely kind. However, taking the justified criticisms to heart, the following week I brought the saddle stand into the shop; and devoted one box window to a first class display of riding equipment. Still, I have to say that one of the nicest tributes came from Mrs Kedwards (nee Bailey). She said: "I think this shop would make my father very happy".

NEW SHOP OPEN TO-DAY (Friday)

T. BECKETT (SADDLER) Ltd.

LEADING SPORTS OUTFITTERS — TRAVELWARE
STABLE and KENNEL REQUISITES

BUSINESS TRANSFERRED TO

43 WOOD STREET
(4 doors away from present premises)

Tel. Stratford-on-Avon 2733   We welcome customers old and new

---

An advertisement in the local newspaper proudly proclaiming
the opening of the new shop at 43 Wood Street.

For a couple of weeks after the opening of the front shop, work was still going on behind the scenes. Our final vacation of 45a Wood Street took place on 21 September, the day the lease expired. The task of transferring all the ledgers from the old office to the new one and carrying hundreds of boxes in cartons from the cellar of the old shop to the new storeroom was more tiring and less exciting than trading lovely merchandise in the shop.

Storage of the goods had to be organised. Our predecessor had used the cellar for ripening bananas. We considered using it to store such items as brass broom-heads and stable buckets. However, when we consulted one of our builders about the possibility of using the cellar for storage, he made a grimace and said: "Well, one of our fellows left a pair of boots down there one day; when he went to collect them the following morning, they were green!"

The workroom furniture - stools, benches, saddle-trees, clams, etc. - were all brought from the Henley Street side of the old premises, down the alley, through the passage and across the yard.

Our saddler, Arthur Trotman, approved of his new workroom. He was really happy when the old clock - bearing the letters round the face *Eliman's Embrocation* - was fixed on the wall of his new abode. This treasure dated back to the William Hyatt period.

At 45a Wood Street, goods had been delivered into the shop. It took some time to train our good railwaymen to use the side passage at 43 Wood Street for large consignments. One day, I was quite shattered when a tough-looking young fellow hauled a large tea chest into the front entrance of the shop. "Want it in here?" he shouted cheerfully. "Oh, no, no, round the side entrance, please."

I took him along the alley, up the passage, and into the stockroom. As I signed for the goods, he promised to tell the staff at the station of the new arrangement.

Some people were confused by the move. Customer habits of 21 years were not easily broken. They automatically made for the old shop and were surprised to find it closed. They could not believe that the move had happened so quickly and smoothly. One dear lady who had been a regular customer of Baileys was most perturbed. "Where do we get the wreaths now?" she cried.

The odd thing was that the upper wall in the alley that had not been demolished still bore witness to the previous Bailey ownership. In fact, the words painted on the brickwork are still discernible.

```
┌─────────────────────┐
│  ┌───────────────┐  │
│  │  H BAILEY     │  │
│  │  FLORIST      │  │
│  │  WREATHS      │  │
│  │  CROSSES      │  │
│  │  MADE         │  │
│  │  TO ORDER     │  │
│  └───────────────┘  │
└─────────────────────┘
```

The first week in October, the shopfitters moved into 45a Wood Street to prepare for the new tenants. One of our dear old customers came into town. She made straight for the old shop, saw the window was cleared, then stood in the middle of the pavement and exclaimed: "Good gracious, Beckett's have gone bankrupt".

She charged into the shop, glared at the gentleman who was organising the shop-fitting and demanded: "Where is it?" Very politely and patiently he asked: "Where is what, Madam?" "My riding saddle," she barked. He explained that we had moved just along the street. Mrs Gee was furious: "How dare they move from here?"

I was in the office one day when a familiar, booming voice sounded in my ears: "How dare you move shop without consulting me?"

Imagine my delight when I set eyes on my old friend, Baliol Holloway, and heard a welcome "Woof!" from Joey. He hardly recognised his new Saville Row tailors!

CHAPTER SEVENTEEN

Sheila Warr

Sheila Warr was recommended to us as an assistant by the local youth officer. She was an attractive, quietly-spoken 16-year-old school-leaver. She needed little training in salesmanship, having a natural aptitude for the job, and an instinctive appreciation of quality merchandise. She seemed, from the outset, to share my reverence for leather and good work-manship. Coming from a farming background, Sheila was not unfamiliar with the needs of farmers and the horse-riding fraternity. The fact that she was with us for eight years, and left only to marry John Lilwall, I think speaks for itself.

Sheila shared my enthusiasm for window-dressing. She was artistic and never lacking in original ideas. Specialist window displays were geared to certain themes, according to the seasons. Easter; a black and gold colour scheme for Shakespeare's birthday; Cruft's; holidays; Pony Club Week; Wimbledon; the Royal Show; Back to School; and Christmas.

We stocked a tremendous variety of belts, many of the fashion models had exquisite buckles. One week we devoted a box window exclu-sively to belts. Our caption being: BELT UP AT BECKETT'S. And they did!

Beautiful luggage practically displayed itself. I remember we stocked a set of ocelot luggage. With little effort on my part, it enhanced the big window and attracted much attention. I think it was the jungle effect that gave it so much appeal. Then a lady came in and bought the beauty case. I hope my lack of enthusiasm did not offend her. It was not like me to be reluctant to make a sale. But it did spoil my display!

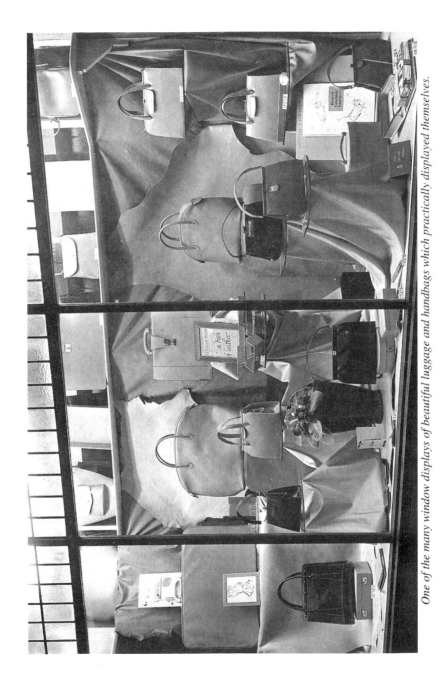

One of the many window displays of beautiful luggage and handbags which practically displayed themselves.

Sheila Warr (second from left) pictured in the new shop with (left to right) Edith Beckett, the author and a representative from one of the suppliers.

Sheila and I spent hours discussing and planning our Christmas window displays, endeavouring to vary the presentation and colour scheme from year to year.

Our customers often sought our advice when choosing gifts for weddings, anniversaries and birthdays. If we could diplomatically discover the name of the boy or girl who was coming of age, we kept a list to save the customer from duplicating the gift - at least from our shop. It worked remarkably well and was much appreciated.

In the winter we did not appreciate the enclosed yard behind the shop. It was not much fun having to go out in the cold to collect goods from the store. However, in the summer this same little area, open to the sky, was a boon. We often took turns to sneak out for a few minutes in the sun, during our coffee or tea break. (Very unofficial - we were not ruled by the unions.)

On a sweltering hot day a rep, very correctly dressed in a smart city suit, would come into the shop and hand his visiting card to Sheila. He was duly shown, not into a business-like office and offered a hard chair, but into the back yard, where an extra garden chair had been hastily placed for him. Long before his order pad was filled, he had shed his jacket, loosened his tie, rolled up his immaculate white shirt-sleeves, and slumped a little deeper into his chair.

We became quite popular with the reps. From the "grapevine" we learned that they enjoyed taking their orders under these somewhat unconventional conditions, in a relaxed atmosphere, in the open air.

The beakers of coffee or tea, according to the time of day, were also welcome.

Next to the yard was the workroom where all the saddlery and leatherwork was carried out. The saddler was Arthur Trotman, who had been with us since Father had taken over the business from Harold Fry in 1932. Tom Goode, our expert saddle repairer, had died in 1943, while we were still at 45a Wood Street. The death of Arthur Trotman really marked the end of an era in that repairs were no longer carried out on Beckett's premises. The workroom was finally closed and turned into a storeroom.

CHAPTER EIGHTEEN

Father's Deteriorating Health

Father found a new interest when he became a member of the Stratford-upon-Avon Rotary Club. He was proposed by Mr Earp, of Earp and Badger. He used to look forward to the weekly Monday luncheons, sharing food and fellowship with his business and professional friends.

Sadly, however, Thomas Beckett was not to enjoy many years working in his beautiful new shop. He had a heart condition that gradually slowed him down. During the latter years of his life, his visits to the shop became less frequent and of shorter duration. He tired quickly. At home, he gave us several scares. When he was fighting for breath, the only person he wanted was his trusted and beloved friend and medical adviser, Doctor McWhinney. "Send for Mac," he would gasp.

Mac never failed to respond. Father had complete confidence in his doctor and it was justified. By 1956 there was little improvement in his cardiac condition. Although he had to limit his activities, Father sadly missed the Monday Rotarian luncheon; it meant so much to him.

In the Spring of 1957, the big talking point at the club was the forthcoming Rotary International Conference to be held in Lucerne from 19-23 May. Father set his heart on joining the Stratford contingent for this special event. His health was deteriorating, but he valiantly worked on extending his little walk down Evesham Road (we moved to Evesham Road in 1955) each day to gain strength. His mental goal was Lucerne. We, his family, did not attempt to deter him. We should have been deeply concerned at his venturing on this trip if we had not known that he would be surrounded by friends who would take care of him. Neither would he be deprived of his medical adviser. Dr McWhinney would be travelling with the Rotarians and could be trusted to keep an eye on Tom.

He made it. At 69 years of age, he was the senior member of the group and received all the kindness and consideration that, not only his seniority, but his gentle nature evoked. His particular guardian angel on this expedition was Rotarian Dick Knight's wife, affectionately known by her friends as "Doll". Father loved telling the story of how he wandered off on his own one day and got lost in the streets of Lucerne.

It was Doll who first missed him, and organised the search party. She practically wept with relief as she flung her arms around him when he was found. She was a lovely lady and, as far as Father was concerned, protective.

He returned from his trip rather pale and exhausted, but there was a new light in his eyes. He had a great sense of achievement. The Lucerne experience had given him confidence. Hence, when names were being submitted for the Autumn Bournemouth Conference, Father was feeling adventurous again and happily joined the Rotarian fellowship.

From the photograph taken at the conference, it seems obvious he was taking a keen interest in the proceedings, and entering into the spirit of the debate. He was content to be flanked by his friends, Mac and Dick. This was his last major outing. Could he make the next goal?

Flanked by his friends Dr 'Mac' McWhinney (left) and Dick Knight, Thomas Beckett is pictured at the Rotarian's Bournemouth Conference.

He was determined to reach the Biblical-allotted span of three score years and ten. This he did on 28 December, 1957.

A new year. What was in store for us? Would Father regain his strength?

Among the many enquirers who shared our concern about Father's deteriorating health was our dear old friend, Baliol Holloway. On 7 January I received this kindly letter from him.

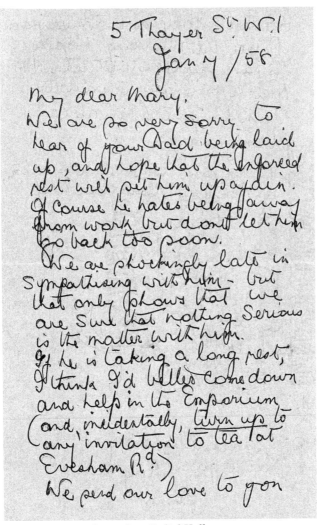

Letter from Baliol Holloway.

As requested, I kept him informed. I conveyed to him our relief and hope when Father seemed much better and well on the road to recovery.

Following a good progress report, on 14 March Bay wrote: 'Thank-you for the good news. I hope you and your mother will not allow him to go down to Wood Street and start throwing his weight around. I wouldn't put it past him.' Then he added 'He's got to loaf about in his slippers. (I shan't even order a new suit for Joey) and when the warm weather comes, a comfortable chair in the garden, I think, and some elevating literature.'

Alas, the improvement did not last. By the early months of 1958, it was apparent that the years had taken their toll. Father became more fragile and, on 3 May, he quietly gave up the struggle.

Those of my readers who have experienced a death in the family will understand what I mean when I say that the days between the death of a loved one and the funeral have a nightmarish quality. It is a period in which a kind of merciful anaesthetic enables you to go through the normal routine, while your heart is breaking. Somehow it is the funeral that marks the real finality of life. For us the days between were strange and unreal. My sister, Jean, came over from Birmingham on the Sunday, but had to return for nursing duty on the Monday evening at the hospital where she worked. We shared the practical tasks that had to be faced. The visits to the Registrar; to the surgery to collect the Death Certificate; to Lodders, the solicitors; and to the florist. Then arrangements for the funeral had to be made with Mr Booker.

However, at the shop, it was business as usual - Father would have wished it. As Sheila swept the shop floor, the tears were streaming down her face. Sheila really loved Father and he loved her.

I went to Foxes to order a printed notice to tell our customers that the shop would be closed the following day for the funeral. I half welcomed, half dreaded the kindly sympathy from customers and friends who met me when I returned to the shop. Some dear people had just slipped into the office and left posies of spring flowers on the table.

Jean came home again on the Tuesday. We tried to save Mother as much as we could, but she was amazing. She quietly settled down and chose hymns for the funeral service: *In heavenly love abiding, Through the love of God our Saviour all will be well, The sands of time are sinking.*

She also decided on the inscription for the headstone.

**To fall asleep is not to die,
To live with Christ is better life.**

We had a lilac tree growing in the tiny yard behind the shop. It was not our tree. It was planted the other side of the wall in the plot belonging to Organs, the furnishers. We had the advantage of it. By climbing out of the upper stockroom window on to the flat roof, we could help ourselves to the lilac. The day before the funeral, Jennifer, our junior assistant, cleared the big shop window. Then Sheila draped it with lilac blue and gold curtains. The drapes concealed three pedestals. I went up to the flat roof and gathered an armful of lilac. We arranged the flowers in three black vases and placed them on the pedestals. I arranged pansies and spring flowers in two small vases and placed them either side of the notice. When I thankfully locked the shop door that night, I stood back and viewed the window. It was really beautiful. The perfume from the lilac still hung in my nostrils.

CHAPTER NINETEEN

The Funeral

As we drew up at the church in Birmingham Road, I remember seeing Father's friend, Freddie Kitchen, standing at the front porch clutching two stacks of extra hymn books. I shall never forget the service. It was wonderful. It was conducted with great dignity and feeling by our Minister and close friend, the Rev. Raymond Ball. The body of the church was filled with Rotarians. The sound of all those male voices singing was awe-inspiring. When it came to the last line of *Through the love of God our Saviour all will be well* I sang with an almost unwonted fierceness: *All must be well.*

It just had to be. Even now, the singing of the hymn *The sands of time are sinking* tugs at my heart. When it comes to the refrain *Glory, glory dwelleth in Emmanuel's land* my eyes become suspiciously moist.

As the coffin was taken into the church, the old corporation horse came along. It stopped. The driver removed his cap. The horse, who had received many a lump of sugar from Mr Beckett's hand, bowed his head.

What fitting tributes to the Master Saddler!

Father was not only respected, he was greatly loved. This was brought home to us again and again, often from unexpected quarters. A short time after the funeral, one of our reps called for his stock order. I thought "I wonder if he knows? But surely he will have read of Father's death in the trade journal?" Then suddenly, he said brightly "How's your father?" I couldn't answer for a moment. When I managed to tell him, I felt cruel. Tears came into his eyes; he looked distraught.

"Oh dear, I have lost an old friend," he said unsteadily. Yes, even the reps shed tears for him.

The lad with the limp devoted his working life to building up a thriving business, supporting the needs of those who enjoyed active sports, in which he himself could never hope to participate. The limp was almost part of his personality. He was recognised by it.

A few days after the funeral, Tom's friend, Dick Knight, came into the shop. "I dreamt about Tom last night," he said. "He was walking towards me when I noticed. 'Tom, you're not limping.' He smiled 'No, Dick. There are no cripples here.'"

EPILOGUE

After the death of Thomas Beckett, his daughter, Mary, took over the full responsibility of running the business. She loved the sales side of the shop, but never really enjoyed the office work that had been her father's domain. She had excellent staff, but there were times when she found the pressures of management burdensome and rather lonely.

Then, nine years later, on 2 July, 1967, Mary and her mother were involved in a serious road accident. How true was the caption in the *Stratford-upon-Avon Herald* 'Lucky to be alive'. The car was a write-off, but miraculously Mary, who was the driver, and her mother survived.

Jean obtained compassionate leave from her nursing post at Sorrento Maternity Unit in Birmingham to nurse the patients after they were discharged from Warwick Hospital. During the three-month period, while her sister was recuperating, she took over the management of the shop.

Soon after, Mary was back and fit for duty again. And she was overjoyed when Jean, who revelled in figures and book-keeping, proposed to leave her profession and go into the business, sharing the responsibility of management.

Edith Beckett made a remarkable recovery from her ordeal, but six years later, at the age of 83, she died on 9 October, 1973. Hence, the surviving two directors of T. Beckett (Saddler) Ltd continued trading in the tradition established by Thomas Beckett until they retired on 17 September, 1979, finally bringing to an end T. Beckett (Saddler) Ltd after 47 years of business.